365 THINGS
TO MAKE YOU GO

HMM

D1039325

A year's worth of class thinking

sparky teaching*

i Independent Thinking Press

First published by

Independent Thinking Press
Crown Buildings, Bancyfelin, Carmarthen, Wales, SA33 5ND, UK
www.independentthinkingpress.com
Independent Thinking Press is an imprint of Crown House Publishing Ltd.

British Library Cataloguing-in-Publication Data
A catalogue entry for this book is available
from the British Library.

Print ISBN: 978-178135115-4
Mobi ISBN: 978-178135157-4
ePub ISBN: 978-1781385158-1
ePDF ISBN: 978-178135159-8

Printed and bound in the UK by
Gomer Press, Llandysul, Ceredigion

*For our wonderful parents
Colin and Jean, Keith and Sheila.*

CHOOSE YOUR OWN ADVENTURE ...

Now that you've opened the book
you are instantly faced with a decision –
where do you go next?

If you are a teacher,
turn to page 8.

If you are a parent, we hope you enjoy going through these with your child.
Turn to page 8, ignoring any jargon you come across along the way,
or just go directly to page 23.

If you are a young person, feel free to skip the next few pages.
For best results, find someone else to discuss your ideas with and see what they
think about each question – it makes things a lot more interesting.
Dive straight into page 23.

If you're the sort of person who reads the last page of the story first, here's a
spoiler: most of the questions here haven't got a specific answer,
but for those that do we've put a few on page 165.

If you don't read small print,
go straight to 365 THINGS TO MAKE YOU GO HMMM on page 23.

INTRODUCTION

Apparently, Hull City is the only team in the football league whose name contains no letters you can colour in[1] (unless you're in Year 7, in which case you'll see an immediate opportunity in the sixth letter).

Fascinating as that fact is, this book doesn't provide you with a year's worth of similarly useless-but-strangely-captivating trivia or general knowledge questions. Hopefully, *365 Things To Make You Go Hmmm ...* is slightly more than that. This is a collection of thought-provoking questions, activities and ideas chosen carefully to help you do four things:

1. Nurture a questioning culture in class. Or, more accurately, a questioning culture amongst your students in your classroom.
2. Encourage openness.
3. Develop your relationship with your class/child.
4. Encourage a range of skills, including:
    a. problem-solving
    b. mathematical thinking
    c. logical thinking
    d. literacy skills
    e. creative thinking
    f. personal and inter-personal skills
    g. a sense of awe and wonder about the world

In short, this book tries to tread a line between interesting and important.

---

1 There's no truth in the rumour that the reason Assem Allam (current Hull City owner) wants to change their name to Hull Tigers is because it would bring the letters 'g' and 'e' to the table.

If you are a teacher, the idea is that you carve out a minimum of five minutes every day with the sole aim of discussing that particular day's question. This could be during registration, at the end of the day or during snatched moments with your class.

Of course, you might want to use them more specifically. Some would serve well as lesson starters (#083), plenaries (#074) or mid-lesson activities to introduce a change of pace. Others deserve more time, so could be worked into a main lesson. You might decide #009 merits an entire maths lesson, #025 would make a great English session or a full Circle Time should be devoted to reflecting on #306. To help you with all of this, some of the questions have been indexed into categories on page 177.

A CASE STUDY

Worth mentioning is the way that Eirian Painter introduced and now uses this with the children at Liberty Primary School in Merton, London. It's an excellent model if you're looking for a way to embed these sorts of questions across your whole school.

Each week, one question is decided on and then announced to the school during assembly. Every classroom then has a poster of the 'Hmmm', as well as one on the school's 'Challenge of the Week' display board.

During the week, specific time is allocated for pupils to respond to the question. They do so by writing their response or answer on colour-coded paper (one each for Early Years, KS1 and KS2) and posting it into the 'Challenge Box' attached to the main display.

The challenge is discussed during Friday's whole-school celebration assembly and one answer from each phase is read out as the winner.

Each week's challenge (and all its responses) is finally filed in a cabinet beneath the Challenge display and the school is steadily building up a powerful library of evidence of the way that children think across the age ranges.

> *Using weekly challenges in this way has encouraged our students to think things through more, rather than accepting a common answer. It's a really useful way for them to deepen their knowledge and understanding of the world.*
>
> Eirian Painter, Deputy Head Teacher, Liberty Primary School, Merton

With their challenge, Liberty have developed the idea to serve the whole school. If only we'd thought of it, this would have been a lot quicker to write – 52 questions would have made a thinner book!

Although we've done our best to make this book as aesthetically pleasing as possible, its real worth doesn't lie in the questions themselves. It's your follow-up questions and the ensuing discussion that will make all the difference. This is a working document.

So, with this in mind, we'd like you to do something. Turn to page 182 and write down a quote you've heard recently that makes you think.

Come back when you've finished ...

Like the best lesson plans, evaluations and Individual Education Plans, this book is much more useful if you view it as a work-in-progress. Please write in it. Highlight sections. Jot down how you've used follow-up questions to develop ideas. Note down inspiring quotes, new stories or website links. Let it become a journal – a home for your Hmmms.

365 IS JUST THE BEGINNING.

THE LIFE CYCLE OF A HMMM-ING BIRD

Spring 2008 – The egg of an idea

365 Things started life as a classroom display. It featured enlarged photos of the heads of students with thought bubbles above each one. They then wrote the questions that were concerning/interesting them at that point in time. 'I know what you should call it,' said one student on their way out to lunch. 'Things that make us go "Hmmm".' And so it began.

June 2009 – Sparky Teaching hatched

Sparky Teaching was created as a home on the web for teachers, parents and students who cared about creative teaching, creative learning and what we believed was the important stuff. Wherever you are in the world, many of the issues teachers face are the same. How can we find opportunities to emphasise character-based values when faced with an increasingly content-heavy curriculum? Is creativity being crowded out of the school day? Through slightly left field – but nonetheless incredibly important – resources, we tried to meet the needs of creatively-minded teachers and parents who didn't mind doing things slightly differently in order to get learning to stick.

September 2009 – **365 Things flew solo**

We started posting one big question every day to get students thinking and sharing their answers. Over the next few years, popularity steadily grew and we did our best to make the content as engaging as possible. To keep things fresh, we deleted the questions and started from #001 again at the end of each year. Every day a new question is still posted at http://sparkyteaching.com/resources/thinkingskills/hmmm.php and tweeted using the hashtag #HmmmsTheWord.

March 2013 – **Some tweeting**

After several tweets, emails and meetings with Ian Gilbert and Independent Thinking Press, it was decided that 365 Things To Make You Go Hmmm … might work well on paper as well as pixels.

June 2014 – **The final migration**

And so here we are. From classroom display, to website, to book. It's been our intention to come up with something that is more intriguing and Hmmm-inducing than the website. Hopefully we've succeeded.

Question Questions

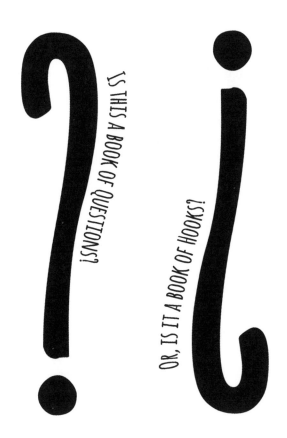

IS THIS A BOOK OF QUESTIONS?

OR, IS IT A BOOK OF HOOKS?

sparky teaching

How many questions get asked in your classroom every day?

In 1912, Stevens stated that approximately eighty percent of a teacher's school day was spent asking questions to students. More contemporary research on teacher questioning behaviors and patterns indicate that this has not changed. Teachers today ask between 300-400 questions each day (Leven and Long, 1981)[1].

Research by Littlewoods[2] found that children ask their mothers between 140 and 390 questions a day, depending on their age and gender.

Of course, you didn't need that data to know the following:

- Young people are innately curious.
- As teachers, we have a tendency to ask too many questions (many of which can be wasted – closed, rhetorical, misdirected or orders disguised as questions).
- If every member of our class asked questions at mother-rate, we'd be in trouble.
- Children tend to open up more (and therefore ask more questions) when they're on their own or in smaller groups.

Who asks the most questions in your classroom?

How can we redress the balance of question power?

What opportunities can we give to our students to ask their own questions?

How can we ensure that those questions arise naturally, out of curiosity?

1 Brualdi Timmins, Amy C. (1998). Classroom Questions. Practical Assessment, Research & Evaluation, 6(6).
2 <http://www.telegraph.co.uk/news/uknews/9959026/Mothers-asked-nearly-300-questions-a-day-studyfinds.html>.

Picture yourself planning for a lesson that's going to be observed. It is easy sometimes to almost decide the questions you want your students to ask beforehand. 'I need them to ask this. And this.' As someone once said, 'I adore spontaneity. Providing it's carefully planned.'

Perhaps if our lesson plans had a blank section for recording great questions that cropped up, it would show that, although we'd given it some thought, we didn't have a definite line of enquiry we wanted students to go down. Instead, we could look forward to seeing what gems they came up with. Obviously, many classes need a little pointer or five, but don't make this your default setting.

That sort of attitude would be really conducive to learning (and surely more impressive to anyone who had the good fortune to observe such a flexible practitioner in action).

How can we ensure that the questions our students ask are high-level ones? Should we be modelling good questioning techniques?

Spray questions around because some of them will hit the mark or limit yourself with a more direct, but risky, approach?

Can we think of them as arrows? We step up to the mark with a limited number in our quiver and each question we use cannot be wasted. They have to be insightful and precise.

When was the last time you stood in front of your class and started a sentence with, 'What would happen if ... ' and you didn't know the answer already?

There's an argument for us to be more genuine in our use of questions – more open about our own lack of knowledge. Despite the government's best intentions, teaching is becoming less about standing at the front and telling a class what to know and more about standing next to them, facilitating their own independent learning.

Which reveals ignorance more: 'I don't know' or 'I've never thought about that'?

{ I WANT TEACHERS TO WONDER OUT LOUD – TO ASK QUESTIONS THAT THEY DO NOT PERHAPS KNOW THE ANSWER TO. } PETER H. REYNOLDS
Author and illustrator

Wonder, Wonder and Wander

A To Do List
For Your Classroom

WOW! WONDER MORE. ☐

WONDER MORE. ☐

WANDER MORE. ☐

Three words. Two sounds. One letter difference. And they adeptly sum up something very special about the best classrooms. The most investigative, stimulating classrooms are those that are awe-inspiring, encourage young people to question the world and are not afraid to meander off the beaten lesson plan if it's worth doing so.

sparky teaching

The combination of allowing yourself to be amazed by the world and asking questions about it should lead to opportunities to digress productively from your planned outcomes. The key word in that sentence is *productively*. Allowing yourself to be led off on a tangent isn't a great character trait to have as a teacher. Controlling that tangent is better.

> We can create learning that places the child at the centre of the action where much of what happens can emerge through a supportive classroom climate, clever questioning and irresistible lures.
>
> Hywel Roberts, *Oops! Helping children learn accidentally* (Independent Thinking Press, 2012)

Teach What Counts

What matters in your classroom?

It's easy to answer that question with all sorts of worthy answers about the things that count to you or the things that you know should count.

But what if your students were consulted? What would they say if they were asked, 'What matters most to your teacher? What do they talk about most? What messages do they send out?' It might not be what you'd hope.

{ We've got 15 weeks until SATs. } **Year 6 Pupil**
Overheard during first week of January 2014

Given that very few 11-year-olds have calendars where they're excitedly crossing off the days until their end-of-year tests, it's probably safe to say that the above quote originated from their teacher (or, more accurately, from an education system that piles pressure onto schools to achieve certain SATs results).

15 weeks is more than a quarter of a year. What sort of message are we giving our students when we greet them back after Christmas with a 105-day countdown?

Something like this?

'What matters in this classroom is the level you get in your SATs because for the majority of your final year here – when you're at the peak of your time at primary school – you'll be keeping half an eye on a couple of hours in May.'

And yet we've all done it. It's incredibly easy to fall into this trap – spending more time at parents' evenings talking about the test scores than the child, starting the term referring to the exams that are coming at the end of it and sending out the message: 'In this classroom what you achieve is more important than who you are.'

Is it, though?

{ NO ONE EVER SAID: 'THIS CHILD OF MINE, MY FONDEST WISH [FOR THEM] IS TO ACE STATEWIDE BENCHMARK MATHS AND SCIENCE TESTS WHEN THEY ARE 16.' } PETER H. BENSON
Psychologist

{ NOT EVERYTHING THAT CAN BE COUNTED COUNTS AND NOT EVERYTHING THAT COUNTS CAN BE COUNTED. } UNKNOWN

Whoever came up with the above aphorism[1], it's a precise one and it's a good one. The big things in life are generally difficult to evaluate. How do you put a percentage on happiness or a value on family?

It takes a brave teacher to tell their students this, though.

Last year, in amongst the encouraging tweets and comments to A level students on results day, one sentence stood out. At first it seemed blunt and unsympathetic, but on a second look it was so true. It went something like this:

'Whether you've got all A grades or failed the lot, don't listen when people say it doesn't matter. It does.'

It took a double take to realise that the author wasn't heartless at all and to understand what he was getting at: what matters is how you react to what you get. Where do you go from here? How resilient are you when faced with failure?

---

1 Apparently not Einstein – who, as is often the case, has been given the dubious pleasure of being cited as its creator.

Surely, we have two roles: academic and pastoral. The first is to raise academic achievement; the second is to develop character, embed important values for life and build self-esteem. The first can be counted, but it's hard to give a value to the second.

The first is reflected in a league table or a graph. The second is reflected in the decisions your students will go on to make.

Success with the first will make us feel like we've won on results day. We may never know how much we've succeeded with the second. Are you okay with that?

Arguably, though, the second will stand our students in better stead for life than the first.

Why was your favourite teacher ever your favourite teacher ever?

As a little experiment, we recently put this question out as a not-so-random straw poll. Here were some of the answers ...

{ A JEWEL OF A TEACHER. WE RESPECTED HIM 100% BECAUSE
HE MADE IT ABSOLUTELY CLEAR THAT HE RESPECTED US. } BRIAN MOSES
Peformance poet and percussionist

{ MY FAVOURITE TEACHER LET ME EXPLORE, CREATE AND
PUSHED ME TO EXCEL. THEY BELIEVED IN MY POTENTIAL. } @MRSOCLASSROOM

{ HE BELIEVED I COULD DO IT WHEN NO ONE ELSE DID,
NOT EVEN ME. } @LISAVENESS

{ MY P6 TEACHER TOLD ME 'EVERYONE IS GOOD AT SOMETHING'.
THAT GAVE ME CONFIDENCE IN MYSELF AND STILL GUIDES
HOW I TEACH TODAY. } @SCOTTISHLASS207

{ HE LET ME MAKE MISTAKES IN THE CLASSROOM
SO THAT I WOULD NEVER BE AFRAID TO MAKE THEM IN THE REAL WORLD. } @CARLASHCROFTHQ

These are interesting in two ways. Firstly, they are evidence that the things people appreciate years later about their teachers are often character-related. Building self-esteem, taking an interest, showing belief – these things last. Secondly, try reading them as a checklist for what makes a great teacher. Are you that kind of person? Teaching isn't a popularity contest, but we would argue that the things that count most in your classroom should be things that still count most years later.

These aren't twenty-first-century skills. People in the first century had to be resilient, creative, flexible and so on. And try to avoid the term 'soft skills' too ...

> *I'm beginning to think that 'soft skills' is a complete misnomer. What exactly is 'soft' about being able to demonstrate resilience, leadership, integrity, confidence, independent thinking and compassion? What is 'soft' about having the skill to communicate, to keep actively learning and adapting to the world around you?*
>
> Hilary French, President of Girls' Schools Association, from the President's Address at the GSA Conference, 2013

To extend this idea, the skills involved in developing character now are exactly the same skills that Abraham Lincoln needed to become president or Nelson Mandela needed to forgive his captors and unite a country. When Nelson Mandela passed away, it was noticeable that the majority of tweets spoke of characteristics that sound fairly ordinary (gentleness, gracious-ness) rather than his extraordinary achievements.

Whether you teach youngsters in a New York kindergarten or history students in a Lancashire secondary school, try and take the time to build these skills into your lessons. Character matters.

NOTICE THINGS

When asked what he does for a living, Seth Godin, the US author, public speaker and entrepreneur, often says, 'I notice things.'

Should you be looking for a class motto for the next 365 days,[1] we'd argue that this is actually quite a robust one ...

WE NOTICE THINGS.

Think about those three words for a second. Stick them on your door and they inform visitors (and your students as they enter it every day) that your classroom is all about finding new information, investigating, pattern-spotting, asking questions, appreciating the world, a sense of wonder, looking for answers and (if you think in terms of noticing each other's feelings) empathy. Mathematical thinking is covered by investigating ideas, noticing patterns and looking for rules we can attribute to them. A 'noticing' classroom is a creative one too, identifying ways to think about and do things differently.

As for you, as teacher, these three words might imply that you try to plan open-ended lessons where students ask the questions and investigate for themselves. And if the lesson takes a slight detour in subject matter, then you're confident enough to recognise value when it's there and go with it. Why? Because your students don't just notice things between 10.00 and 10.25 on Tuesdays. Intrigue and wonder can strike at any moment and generally don't obey the rules of last night's lesson plan.

---

1 If you're not convinced by the need to have a class motto, have a read of Stephen Lockyer's blog: <http://www.classroomtm.co.uk/branding-your-classroom/>. Branding your classroom isn't a fun little primary school activity (although it is fun and would work brilliantly at primary school level). It's about giving your students that feeling of togetherness and that they're part of a team, giving them a desire to work together for its aims.

'We notice things' says, 'We're intrigued. We're curious. We question. We take an interest. We discover, observe and detect. Apathy is not what we're about.'

We're sure Mr Godin wouldn't mind you appropriating the concept for your classroom door ...

If he asks, just say you noticed it somewhere.

Think On ...

We're differentiating our teaching more and more at the same time as standardising tests more and more. Are the two things compatible?

What is it about your teaching that you wish inspectors could see, but they never do?

You're being observed tomorrow. Do you plan backwards from a checklist of what makes an outstanding lesson or forwards from a checklist of how your students will learn best? Or are the two the same?

If everyone was graded outstanding, would it make sense?

Are terms like 'thinking skills', 'values' and 'big questions' wishy-washy, unquantifiable nonsense?

'We're teachers, not life coaches. Grades matter.' Discuss.

Start Small. Think Big.

{ A FULLY-INCLUSIVE CLASSROOM ASKS QUESTIONS SMALL ENOUGH FOR ALL TO CONSIDER AND OPEN ENOUGH TO EXPAND TO ANY LEVEL. } @JosephHFuller

? Allow the simplest of things to start you wondering ...

#001

When does a human being first begin to think?

#002

Come up with four ways to draw a sheep that don't actually involve drawing a sheep.

#003

Write the word CONFIDENT where you think it belongs on this character line.

Although lots of you will have written CONFIDENT at the opposite end to SHY, maybe it belongs in the middle, with OVERCONFIDENT or COCKY at the other end. Many of the characteristics we think are opposites can be stretched out a bit more until they become negative. For example, you might think the opposite of being a coward is being brave, but you can stretch out the idea of being brave more and more until you have someone who does things that are actually extremely risky and quite foolhardy.

Can these positive qualities become negative if you stretch them enough?
friendly   careful   ambitious   calm   determined   easy-going   modest

#004

If there was an implant that allowed you to hear everybody's thoughts at all times would you want it? Would it be a blessing or a curse to know what other people were thinking?

#005

You are an art collector who owns the only two paintings left by a famous artist. These are world-famous works of art, hundreds of years old, and incredible precision has gone into every brushstroke. At the moment they are worth a few thousand each. If you destroy one of these beautiful paintings, the remaining painting will be worth millions to you as it will be the last one left in the world.

Would you destroy it?

OOPSY

#006

Awe and wonder are like a couple of sumo wrestlers. Massive things, hard to pin down, but if they ever decide to burst into your classroom they change everything.

What was the last awe-filled moment that stopped you in your tracks?

#007
(Licence to Think)

What skills *that you learn in school* would be useful to a secret agent?

#008

It's possible you've never heard of the name Miles Scott. On 15 November 2013, thousands of people helped the Make-A-Wish Foundation turn San Francisco into Gotham City for a day so that five-year-old Miles (who is recovering from leukaemia) could be Bat Kid. Dressed in a mini Batman costume, he solved several staged crimes, was cheered on by crowds and even got a thank you message for saving the day from Barack Obama! The hashtag #SFBatKid was trending on Twitter for most of the day.

But, do you know what? Miles was a superhero long before 15 November and it had nothing to do with Batman. Many of the most inspiring people this world has to offer are under the age of 18, and the beauty of this fact is they haven't done anything special except be themselves. They've been through a lot – illness, tragedy, difficulties – but they've kept positive and kept going. What makes them amazing is that they stay smiling, even though they've been through things that most of us will never have to deal with.

At the time of writing this we've just read of an 18-year-old boy who hasn't got long to live. His parents wake up not knowing whether each day will be his last. But he doesn't want to waste a moment and has started up his own small business making bird boxes, which he'd like his siblings to take over one day. That kind of

#009

When you're the mother of identical quadruplets how do you tell them apart? Tan Chaoyun from Shenzhen in China answered that question by shaving each of her quadruplets' hair into a different digit: 1, 2, 3 and 4! Today's question won't help Mrs Tan to identify her children any better, but it'll get you thinking. How many different four-digit numbers could they make by sitting in different positions on their school bench?

Some extensions:

- Imagine one of them is off sick. How many different three-digit numbers could they make?
- Now imagine one of their friends goes to Mrs Tan for a haircut too. How many five-digit numbers could the boys make?
- There's a children's book by Margaret Mahy called *The Seven Chinese Brothers*. It's got nothing to do with any of this, but you know what question is coming, don't you?

#010

As this is being typed, somewhere out there China's Jade Rabbit rover is exploring the Moon and the Curiosity rover is still roaming Mars.

Although these news stories have had mentions in the media, in the past everyone would surely have been really excited by them. They would be on the front of every newspaper in town and people would have gathered round their televisions to witness them. Even when Felix Baumgartner successfully skydived from the edge of space, it didn't seem to get as big a reaction as you might expect.

Have we become harder to amaze?[1]

#011

Here's a creative challenge for sparky teachers and their classes.

This week we'd like to learn about .... through the medium of ....

Your job is to fill in the blanks in the sentence above (making sure you agree on one answer as a class).

The first blank should be a topic you are studying in class at the moment. The second can be anything you like that makes sense (rap music, magazines, sculpture, poetry, puppets – almost anything goes!). Your teacher's job is to get creative and come up with a way to introduce or teach that subject using the style that you've suggested. It might not work, but it should provoke some ideas of how to teach your subject in interesting ways.

---

1 After asking this question on the website, we had a reply from a Twitter follower, @Wharfytime, which is worth including here. Have we become harder to amaze? 'I thought so, but I recently showed my kids this video of Curiosity and they were awestruck.' Watch the video – you'll see why: <https://www.youtube.com/watch?v=Ki_Af_o9Q9s&feature=player_embedded>.

012

There are many writers and musicians out there who would appreciate somewhere to go when they run out of ideas. If you ran a creativity surgery where writer's block was cured, what would it be like?

013

You've been commissioned to write *The Survival Guide for Life in this Class.* What are the 10 most important things you think you ought to mention for people to make it through in one piece?

014

'All cars should be made of lightweight plastic.'

What are the strengths and weaknesses of this idea? What would need to change to make the concept work?

015

All the digits in 2014 are different. The next time this will happen is 2015. The last time it happened was 2013! But when was the time before that?

016

You are going to bury a time capsule. It will be opened in the year 3000. What five items would you choose to show future generations what your locality was like way back now?

HOW CAN I RESIST PEER PRESSURE?

#017

What sorts of things are people your age pressured to do?
Is peer pressure always bad?

#018

WHAT'S THE biggest question[1] YOU CAN COME UP WITH?

&

#019
WHAT'S THE
smallest thing
YOU NEED TO
MAKE YOU
happy
?

1 What makes a question 'big' – is it how important the question is? Is it the way the question is asked? Is there such a thing as some questions being bigger than others?

#020

Some people think that if you're having fun, you're not doing anything worthwhile (apart from enjoying yourself). But it's possible to change human behaviour for the better by using fun as an incentive.

A few years ago in Sweden, Volkswagen ran an advertising campaign where they set up little experiments and a competition to show how people's behaviour could be changed by making things more fun. For example, they converted the stairs at a railway station to a set of piano keys. More people wanted to use the stairs instead of using the escalators. Another experiment involved getting people to throw rubbish into 'The World's Deepest Bin' (people threw their empty cans into a bin that made a cartoon falling sound and eventually a splash). Another idea someone came up with was speed camera prizes. The speed camera caught drivers over the speed limit and fined them as usual. But it also recorded good behaviour and, every month, picked some of the good drivers' names and awarded them cash prizes out of the fine pot.[1]

It's definitely true that people are more likely to do things if there is an element of fun involved. Taking this idea into school, how could your teacher influence behaviour by introducing fun to the following activities:

- Revising for exams
- Tidying the classroom
- Completing homework early
- Wearing school uniform
- Putting litter into the bin
- Arriving at school on time

#021

Why do so many bad things happen in the world?

#022

What was your last 'Aha!' moment?

---

1 You can see more of Volkswagen's incentive experiments here: <http://www.thefuntheory.com/>.

023

Which of these amazing facts isn't a fact?

- An anteater's snout is shaped in such a way that if it were able to talk, it wouldn't be able to say the word 'saveloy'.

- If everyone from Norway stood on top of each other's shoulders, they could just reach the moon. Just!

- Officially, the tallest mountain in the world is Mount Everest. Actually, it's not at all. Mount Kilimanjaro in Tanzania is 315ft taller. However, as Kilimanjaro is a dormant volcano it's not officially classed as a mountain and can't be included in the statistics.

- Jocao fruit beetles are found in most Jocao trees. Many of them die off through pesticides and washing, but around 12% of bunches of Jocaos in supermarkets still contain these tiny lovable rogues who have by now burrowed deep inside the fruit. If you've eaten a bunch of Jocaos, you've probably also eaten a fruit beetle or two. Thankfully, they're quite good for you – a good source of protein and actually tastier than the fruit.

#024

What makes a sparky teacher?

#025

The Oulipo movement in France was started by a group of writers and poets who thought they could become more creative by obeying rules in their writing (see #162). Having rules like this is not a lot different to being limited in how many characters to use in a tweet or writing a 50-word story. The Oulipo writers tried things like writing without using certain letters or writing the same story out in lots of different styles.[1] In Raymond Queneau's *Exercises in Style*, he rewrites the same little scene about seeing a man on a bus again and again, using lots of different styles.

So, here's an Oulipo challenge for you ...

Rewrite the opening paragraph of your favourite book using one of the following styles:

1950s detective   angrily   interview   comedy   official letter

#026

If you had to stay one age forever, what age would you choose and why?

P7, St Margaret's Primary, Cowie

#027

You could say your brain is like a sponge because it soaks up lots of information, but it doesn't hold it for very long. What else could you liken your brain to and why?

---

1 Teachers, see the work of Alan Peat if you'd like to use this sort of thing in class. His *50 Ways to Retell a Story: Cinderella* is a particularly good example.

#028

The word STARTLING is the longest word in the English language that still makes a word each time you take away a letter. What are the words?

#029

Is it true that the more times you travel around the sun the wiser you get?

#030

Think of a way to encourage students in your school to be more patient. For example, you could reward those who wait until last for dinner by allowing them to have seconds.

#031

If you're reading late at night, toast isn't a good snack to accompany you because of the crumbs. Can you name four late-night-reading-friendly snacks?

#032

Could you forgive anything if the person was truly sorry?
Should you?

#033

BBC TV show *The Apprentice* features budding entrepreneurs out to impress Lord Sugar. It seems that to feature in the show you need to be good at similes and metaphors saying how fantastic you are ...

> I'M NOT JUST A ONE-TRICK PONY. I'M NOT A TEN-TRICK PONY. I'M A WHOLE FIELD OF PONIES.

STUART BAGGS
The Apprentice, 2011

> I'M LIKE A SHARK. RIGHT AT THE TOP OF THE FOOD CHAIN. I TAKE WHAT I WANT, WHEN I WANT.

RICKY MARTIN
The Apprentice, 2012

Here are some more examples from Miss Thomas's English class at Oldfields Hall Middle School:

IF BUSINESS WAS AN ADVENTURE, I WOULD BE GANDALF ... 'THOU SHALL NOT PASS!'

I'M A GIANT. I'LL WALK OVER EVERYTHING!

I AM LIKE A JELLYFISH. I MAY LOOK QUIET, BUT IF YOU GET IN THE WAY, I'LL STING YOU!

I'M LIKE A SNAKE READY TO ATTACK AND I'M GOING TO SLITHER MY WAY TO THE TOP!

Have a go at writing your own similes and metaphors to sell yourself to a prospective boss – the more outrageous the better! Lord Sugar's search for a decent metaphor has begun.

#034

Where did our amazing planet and everything on it come from?

#035

Do you ever doubt yourself or what you think? Is this okay?

#036

Which are more important: ideas, feelings or things?

#037

Is zero a number?

038

O T T F F S

Which three letters come next in the sequence? Why?

039

When people first started voting to elect their leaders, it was only certain men who were allowed to vote. Over time, that changed – slaves and poorer men were included and eventually, after a real struggle, women won the right to vote too. In most countries the age you are allowed to vote is 18. Many countries have talked about lowering this age limit and some politicians in Germany have even discussed allowing young children to vote. What should the age limit for voting be? If children were allowed to vote, what effects would it have?

040

When are you at your most creative?

Think about time of day, what you're doing, what sounds you like in the background, your posture, where you are ...

Would it be a good idea for your classroom to be a bit more like this?

041

Invitation

YOU ARE INVITED TO INVITE
THREE FAMOUS PEOPLE FROM HISTORY
FOR AN EVENING OF
GOOD FOOD AND GREAT CONVERSATION WITH YOU.

Choose wisely, this is a one-off!

1. _____

2. _____

3. _____

AS AN EXTENSION, COMPARE YOUR CHOICES WITH OTHER PEOPLE'S.
WHAT DOES EACH DINNER GUEST BRING TO THE TABLE?
WHAT DOES THAT SAY ABOUT THE PERSON WHO CHOSE THEM?
ANOTHER IDEA IS TO PUT EVERYBODY'S TRIOS IN A HAT
AND TRY AND GUESS WHO CHOSE THEM.
THEY CAN PROVIDE QUITE AN INSIGHT INTO SOMEONE'S CHARACTER.

042

You are a time traveller and have just arrived from 2080. What three things are going to happen in the year ahead?

043

If you choose an answer to this question at random, what's the chance that you will get it right?[1]

A: 25%   B: 50%   C: 60%   D: 25%

044

If you were to spell out numbers O-N-E-T-W-O and so on, how long would it be before you said the letter Y? What about the letter A?

045

What life skills can computer games teach you? What can't they teach you?

---

1 As seen on Twitter.

> #046

> ' BELIEVE

WHAT YOU LIKE.

> AS LONG AS IT'S TRUE FOR YOU,
THAT'S WHAT MATTERS.'

> DOES THIS MAKE SENSE?

■

WOULD THE WORLD BE BETTER IF WE ALL SPOKE THE SAME LANGUAGE?

Y4, Rickmansworth Park JMI School, Herts

048

If there were a chart for Top Ten Maths Mistakes, what do you think would feature in it? Compare your top ten with a friend. Are there any similar mistakes? What can you do about them?

049

'As long as you've got a calculator (and most mobiles have one nowadays) you don't really need to know a lot of maths – just the basics.'

Try and persuade this person otherwise by coming up with as many interesting answers as possible. It might help to imagine a world without maths.

050

Here's a 10-word story. Can you do better?

Will my disappearing machine work? I'll just press this b

051

Is crying a sign of weakness?

052

Your brain alters all the time.

It's altaring naw as you reid this santonce and wroikng orvetime as it treis to udnrtsnud the typos.

Amnaizgly it can aslo rcegosine wrods wehn the mdidle lttrees are jmbueld up.

W1th @ l1ttl3 cOnc3ntr@t1On, 1t c@n 3v3n m@k3 53n53 Of th15, wh1ch 15 r3@lly 1mpr3551v3!!

Our brains are made up of billions of neurons (brain cells) connected by synapses (like tiny wires). When you learn things and when you remember things, you make connections in your brain. But the cells in your body are changing all the time.

So, where are your memories kept? Also, while we're at it, are all your joys, memories and sorrows nothing but a bunch of electrical signals? Is that all you are?

053

A bike has two wheels, one large and one small. As the rider cycles along, do the wheels travel at different speeds?

054

You are a doctor with a difference. Instead of medicines, your treatment is given by recommending art. Which books, music, poetry, drama or art will you prescribe for a patient who needs inspiring? What about for someone who is sad?

055

Name as many things as you can that are named after animals, but aren't actually animals. How many of them have the characteristics of that animal?

056

As teachers, we're always encouraging you to take risks. But what does risk-taking look like in a classroom where you don't bungee jump or wrestle bears on a daily basis?

057

Are 'learning' and 'being taught' the same thing? If not, what's the difference?

058

What's an average person?

059

Where do right and wrong come from?

060

Shannon and Bailey go for a curry. The bill comes to £25 and they decide to split it equally. They each put in £15.

'Here you go,' says Shannon to the waiter. 'There's thirty pounds there. We'd like you to take a £3 tip out of it as well after we've paid the £25 for the meal.'

The waiter thanks them and takes the £30 to the cashier, who gives him the £5 change for the meal. The waiter then does what Shannon suggests, pockets £3 as the tip and then goes back to the table.

'Here's your change,' he smiles. 'I've taken my £3 out already so there's only £2 left.'

He then hands each of them a pound.

'Hang on,' says Shannon. 'We both paid you £15 to start with and you've just given us each a pound back. So really that means we paid £14 for our meals.'

'Right ... ' the waiter agrees.

'Two fourteens means we spent £28 on the meals,' explains Shannon.

'Ri-i-i-i-ght,' says the waiter, now slightly worried as his maths isn't as good as it used to be.

'And you've got £3 sitting in your pocket as a tip,' Shannon continues. '£28 plus £3 is £31.'

'But we only gave him £30 to start with!' says Bailey.

'I know!' cries Shannon. 'Where on earth did that extra pound come from?'

#061

WHO WOULD YOU GIVE THESE COMPLIMENTS TO?

YOU'RE SO INSPIRING, YOU MAKE ME WANT TO TRY HARDER.

YOU'VE ALWAYS GOT TIME FOR ME. THANK YOU.

YOU ARE ONE OF THE MOST CREATIVE PEOPLE I KNOW.

IF I NEEDED WISE ADVICE, I'D COME AND ASK YOU.

#062

How are colours used in ways that aren't obviously to do with colour? For example, rhythm and blues, black market, in the red ...

#063

When counting sheep doesn't work, can you recommend any good ways of sending yourself to sleep?

#064

Which digit is the most common between the numbers 1 and 1000? And while you're at it, which digit is the least common?

#065

What life lessons could you learn from a seagull?

#066

Without using either word in your answer, what is truth and what is a lie?

#067

Is it okay to keep zoo animals in cages?

#068

Which of these is the odd one out and why?

14 93 32 57

#069

Who decides the price of a pint of milk?

Think carefully.

#070

What problems can't computers solve? Do you think one day they will be able to?

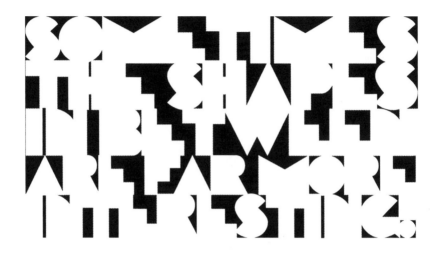

#071

Can you see something more here than shapes on a page? Try and write or draw something using only negative space.

#072

Shane Lynch, former member of the pop group Boyzone, admitted that when he was at school, he used to always sit behind the biggest, naughtiest pupil in the class. He is dyslexic and this was a strategy he used to hide so he'd never be asked a question. If you wanted to avoid being asked questions in your classroom, what tactics would you use? (It might sound like a strange question, but your teacher will find your answers VERY helpful!)

#073

Talent is hiding in your school.[1] Find it.

---

1 In other words there are lots of skills that people don't know about. Your sparks don't always fit neatly into school subjects and so they often don't get seen in school. The person who sits next to you in class might be great at caring for the elderly or mending bikes. Your caretaker might play the saxophone and your school cook might be a chess grandmaster. But, because you never have cause to ask, you'll never know. Root out that talent, and when you find it, celebrate it!

#074

SUM UP THE CONTENT OF YOUR LAST LESSON

IN A TWENTY-SECOND DOODLE

#075

How many countries can you name with only five letters?

P6b, Cornbank St James Primary School, Penicuik

#076

Who or what do you have faith in?

#077

Think of a question that would make you think, 'I wonder who'd ask a question like that!'

#078

Write down any three-digit number with digits that get smaller from left to right. Write down the number backwards. Take the smaller number away from the bigger. Add the answer to the reverse of itself. Your answer should be a four digit number.

Write it here: ___ ___ ___ ___

Take the first three of those digits and find that question number in this book. With the last digit, count that many words into the question. What do you notice?

#079

Has there ever been such a thing as a perfect person? Is anyone completely good?

#080

The advice often given to victims of bullying is usually 'TELL SOMEONE'. But for the person being bullied, that's often a massive step to take. Maybe they don't want to be seen as telling tales or are worried about the repercussions. It's a very real problem. What would you say to someone who is being bullied, but doesn't feel able to tell?

#081

Share some knowledge between the generations. When was the last time you sat down and learned from someone your grandparents' age? When was the last time they learned from you?

#082

What's the most powerful thing anyone can do
with a piece of blank paper and a pen?

#083

Using only the digits in the current year, how many different numbers can you make? You can add, subtract, multiply or divide, but you can only use those four digits once.

#084

Is everybody treated equally in your school? In your country? In the world?

How could the world be made a fairer place?

#085

If you could learn about ANYTHING today, what would you learn?

(The only rule is that you have to be able to justify to your teacher how important it is!)

#086

What do you think the first invention ever was?

087

Can you think of a question that can be answered with a question?[1]

088

Not everyone is very good at maths, reading or writing essays. If you could be tested at anything at all, what would you shine at?

089

Throughout the world there are lots of languages that are gradually dying out.[2] One of these is Tuscarora, which was spoken in Southern Ontario and parts of the United States. Apparently there are only nine native speakers left. In the Tuscarora language, objects are described by using verbs rather than nouns, so when they talk about a black snake they say 'he climbs' and everyone knows what that refers to. A boy is described as 'he is young' and for a goat they say 'it stinks'!

Have a go at converting nouns into verbs in this way. See if others in your class can guess the word from your Tuscarora-style description.

090

Is it okay to try and look older than you actually are?

---

1 The interesting thing about this question is that it's a question that can be answered by a question that can be answered by a question! Even more interestingly, it can also be answered with itself.

2 Apparently someone once wanted to record one of these dying languages to preserve it in written form. The slight problem was that it could never be verified as the two only remaining speakers weren't on speaking terms!

#091

Are you ever truly alone?
Who or what guides you when you are?

LIVE CURIOUSLY.
WRESTLE BIG QUESTIONS.
WONDER MORE.
COLOUR OUTSIDE THE LINES.
MAKE THE BEST OF EVERYTHING.
WANDER MORE.
BE SOMEONE ELSE'S HERO.
HAVE ECLECTIC TASTES.
DOODLE MORE.
BE THE BIGGER PERSON,
FORGIVE BEFORE THEY APOLOGISE.
STOP. COLLABORATE AND LISTEN.
STAND FOR SOMETHING.
BE SPARKY.

© sparky teaching 2013

#092

Name four more alternative rules for your class you think should also have been mentioned. Out of all of these, which is the most important?[1]

---

1 If you like this poster, you might like these: <http://www.sparkyteaching.com/resources/motivational/messagesthatmatter.php>.

#093

Seeing as light has to travel, is everything we look at in the past?

Kahlo Class, Millennium Primary School, Greenwich

#094

Is everything natural, beautiful? Is anything man-made more beautiful than its natural equivalent?

#095

You've been summoned to your head of year's office. Your behaviour has been so bad you will have a detention at some point in the next week (Monday through to Friday).

But, because she wants to give you a chance, she says that you'll only get the detention if she can surprise you with it and you won't be told the day until it arrives. If you know for sure that it is a particular day, she can't surprise you and you won't be punished.

You smile because you know this means you won't have a detention all week. How is this possible?

CLUE: Start with Friday. Can she take you by surprise with a Friday detention? What about Thursday?

#096

Invent a website idea that would help to bridge the gap between generations.

#097

Why are some people so mean?

#098

In 2013, Mike Crates, a fishmonger from South Wales, won the British Fish Craft Championships. He'd been trying for 41 years and came second 20 times. What will YOU keep trying at until you succeed?

#099

What makes someone ready to learn?

#100

Professor Mick Waters[1] and the National Trust have both written lists of activities that all children should have experienced by the age of 11¾. They're very outdoors-based lists, full of action. What would feature on your 'Must-Do' list? (You don't have to have done it, you just have to think it's worth encouraging other people to do.)

An interesting extension would be to put together a 'Must-Know' list too. How many of these things should be done at school?

---

1 Mick talks about this and how it can be used in his excellent book *Thinking Allowed: On Schooling* (Independent Thinking Press, 2013). Recommended highly.

101

BUILD YOUR OWN HERO(INE)

PURELY BASED ON CHARACTER, PUT TOGETHER SOMEONE YOU CAN REALLY LOOK UP TO.

THE RESILIENCE OF

THE KINDNESS OF   THE DETERMINATION OF

THE HONESTY OF   THE CARING NATURE OF

THE CHEERFULNESS OF   THE CREATIVITY OF

THE NEVER-SAY-DIE STICKABILITY OF

#102

'Children should get off their computers and play outside more.'

Be honest, is this true?

#103

How many of these statements do you agree with?

- — When you flip a coin, there's a 50% chance of it landing on heads.
- — When you flip a coin, each time you flip is completely random – it doesn't matter what you flipped before.
- — You've got as much chance of flipping 10 heads in a row as flipping H T H H T T T H T H.

#104

In all of space and time, everything that ever happened and everything that has ever been, where would you visit first if you could? Why?

Matthew, Birch Class, Liberty Primary School, Merton

#105

Come up with 10 strategies for losers. (By which we mean people who constantly lose things – PE kit and homework being two main ones.)

#106

How would you describe the difference between worry, fear and panic?

#107

Your friends' characteristics are ingredients that they bring into your life. What is the most common ingredient they all bring? Does that say something about you?

#108

What is unusual about the number 1089?

#109

What personal e-safety rules do you stick to when you're on the Internet?

#110

An antigram is a word that when you rearrange the letters you can make a new word or phrase that means something very different – in fact, almost the opposite! For example: earliest – rise late.

Rearrange these antigrams to make almost opposite words/ phrases ...

astronomers   funeral   united   honestly   silent   violence
within earshot   forty-five   restful

#111

How is mathematics a language? What about music?

#112

Find someone you respect, someone who always seems to have the answers. Ask them for three questions they don't know the answer to. We all go Hmmm …

#113

Ralph Caplan (a US author who writes about design) once said, 'If more designers had bad backs, we would have more good chairs.'

What do you think he meant by this? What are YOU best placed to design?

#114

What's the bravest thing you've ever heard anyone having done? Do you think everyone has stores of bravery inside them, ready for when it's called upon? Or do you think some people have more than others?

#115

How much of how you feel about yourself is to do with what other people say about you? Is that right? How would you feel about yourself if you were stranded on a desert island, with no one around to comment on you?

It was summertime. Arthur took a lazy stroll across the road. The car behind him could wait. Out of all the other cats on the estate, Arthur was head honcho and, as far as he was concerned, anything in his path had to give way to him. This rule included vehicles, much to the residents' irritation.

He gave the car a cold, hard stare, coughed up a hair ball and wondered how best to spend the rest of the afternoon. The pavement, already nicely warmed by the morning sun, was an inviting possibility. But then there were a couple of magpies who needed to be shown who was boss and he had to collect this week's protection money from that mouse at No.26. Decisions, decisions... He yawned and had a scratch as he contemplated his options. It was lonely at the top.

'OOOWWWWOOOO!!' Suddenly a scream cut through the afternoon air like a chainsaw through cheesecake. Arthur shivered and spun around, his fur standing to attention. What on earth could make such an inhuman sound? Some kind of monster?

"OOWOOOOWOOO!!" Again it came. But this time it was accompanied by four canine legs bounding towards him. Top cat or not, Arthur turned and fled. He was being chased by no ordinary beast.

#116A   AFTER YOU'VE READ IT, SHAKE THIS PAGE ...

lonely | afternoon.

cold, hard | air

like | summertime | shivered and

the morning sun, | had | turned and fled.

was an invit
a scratch
nim. had
st lonely
t then
It a chainsaw through
Top car
d, No.
ecisions,
un c
ound, hi
cur standing to
sound?
me a
such an inhuman
ball
of monste
attention.
he as
as he was
Again it
give
accompanied by four canine
He was being
ed by thur
Arthur
But this
ards him.
"OOOWWWWOOOO!!!"
beast.
narv

#116B   WHAT CAN YOU MAKE BY SHAKING THINGS UP?

#117

AHP FTGR BL "T ZHHZHE"?

#118

There is a clever slogan that talks about being careful about what you post on the Internet. It says something like:

'If it's not true, helpful, inspiring, necessary or kind, then THINK before you post it.' Take that as your inspiration and post something today that could be described by one or more of those words.

#119

'Eureka! I think I've got it! Shoes provide a warm, waterproof covering for our feet, but how about a covering for our feet to go in between our actual feet and the existing covering for our feet? It'll be like an extra layer of foot. I'll make millions,' he said.

'Oh, put a sock in it,' sighed his wife.

Apart from the sock, are there any objects that you just can't quite understand how they were invented?

#120

If it were possible, how many times do you think you would need to fold a piece of paper in half to reach the moon?[1]

---

1 That is a genuine question. Here's a clue: it's either a) 42 times, b) 420 times, c) 4,200 times or d) a number bigger than 42 billion times.

WE HAVE LIFT OFF! PLEASE FOLD HERE.

ANOTHER SMALL FOLD FOR MAN. A GIANT LEAP FOR MANKIND!

REACH FOR THE STARS. KEEP FOLDING ...

It was a normal day at the garage. Rick doodled on an A453(b) payment request as he spoke to a customer on the phone. The A453 (b) were the forms used to request spare parts from local garages and paying a monthly invoice instead of separate transactions. It was by far an easier way to do business particularly in the car maintenance trade.

The pen Rick was using was a blue biro, slightly chewed on one end. The lid had been missing for a while, but it was still working, which was a good thing because it was the last working pen in the office.

Outside, a large parcel van reversed over a drain and the driver got out to check through the day's deliveries. A nearby pigeon played with a Cheese and Onion crisp packet that had escaped the recycling bins.

Wandering the slowly-busying streetwasthe postman, trying to find where Flat 16 was. This was no surprise, as Flat 16 was well-hidden from the road and you could only really get to it if you accessed it from the side-alley.

#121 Is it OK to skip whole sections of a book and fast-forward a DVD if things get particularly boring? Or should you persevere?

Rick sighed as he put the phone down.

"That was Mr Price," he announced. "He's bringing his van in for a service first thing tomorrow."

"First thing?" asked Neville. "But where will he park it?"

"I was wondering that," said Rick. "We've got no space on the forecourt now that we've had to use it for refuelling. I just...."

Suddenly there was an unearthly howl. Rick dropped his pen. The wolves were back.

#122

If you were mixed up with an identical baby when you were born, would it make a difference if you were called the wrong name for the rest of your life?

#123

'Nothing great was ever achieved without enthusiasm.'

How could you increase your enthusiasm levels today?

#124

Can quitters ever win?

You've probably heard the saying, 'Winners never quit and quitters never win.'

But is there a time to say, 'That's it, time to stop,' or should you plough on? If there is such a time, how do you know when that is? If not, will success come in the end?

#125

In which direction is the bus travelling? (The only possible answers are left or right.) Explain your answer.

#126

Here's a special list of qualities:

love, joy, peace, patience, kindness, goodness, faithfulness, gentleness, self-control.

What do these qualities look like in a person? Which one of these qualities do you look for most in a friend?

#127

3 MINUTES   **4 MINUTES**

You've got two egg timers. One times three minutes and the other four minutes.

Using both timers in whichever way you choose, is there a way of timing every possible minute from 1–10?

Some targets you will find easier than others and you may find that you need to do some preparation, but it is possible.

#128

Here are some facts about the French king, Louis XIV.

Born: 1638

Ascended to throne: 1643

Died: 1715

Age at death: 77 years old

And obviously, Louis was the 14th king of France to be called Louis.

There are some amazing coincidences in those numbers if you can spot them. There are four to find and the best way to find them is to do some maths with the digits. Can you spot the numerical coincidences?

#129

Every astronaut who has been into space has come back to
Earth changed. Many of them have commented on how planet
Earth looks so fragile, a little blue dot surrounded by space.

If there's no gravity in space, what keeps our planet hanging
without dropping or floating away?

#130

'It suddenly struck me that that tiny pea, pretty and blue, was the Earth. I put up my thumb and shut one eye, and my thumb blotted out the planet Earth. I didn't feel like a giant. I felt very, very small.'

Neil Armstrong

Right now, that tiny pea is where you are. How do you think looking down on that tiny pea would make you feel?

#131

Are we the only planet with life on it? Is this by chance or design?

#132

In 2013, a lady called Diana Nyad swam from Cuba to Florida. That's a distance of 110 miles (the equivalent of swimming the English Channel just over five times without stopping) and she spent 53 hours swimming it (the equivalent of starting on a Monday morning at 9am and not stopping until Wednesday at 2pm!). She had to deal with strong winds, rough seas, jellyfish and the very real risk of sharks.

The second-best bit of this story is that this was Diana Nyad's fifth attempt at trying over a period of 35 years. The best bit is that she was 64 years old. Here's a quote from this incredible lady: 'You tell me what your dreams are. What are you chasing? It's not impossible. Name it.'

Is she right or are some dreams impossible? (Even though she's such an inspiring lady, you are allowed to disagree with her if you like!)

#133

Once, if someone with nothing better to do with their time wanted to make a nasty comment about you behind your back, they could only do it to an audience of their friends. Now someone can post or tweet a comment about you and hundreds of people can see it in seconds – people who don't know the real you and can't make up their minds for themselves. Reputations and self-esteem can be destroyed by people who don't even have the courage to give their real name. Can anything be done about this or is the only answer 'Don't go on Twitter/Facebook etc.'?

#134

Being able to argue in favour of something that you don't believe is quite a skill. Lawyers have to do it all the time.[1] Explain why you think yoghurt is the greatest discovery man has ever made.

#135

What would it have been like being the first person on earth?

Mr Woodburn's Class, Year 4, Milnthorpe Primary School, Cumbria

---

1 Some people would say politicians are quite good at it too, but that's another story.

78

#136

What are the next two numbers in the sequence?

1, 1, 2, 3, 5, 8, __, __

What have these numbers got to do with this illustration?

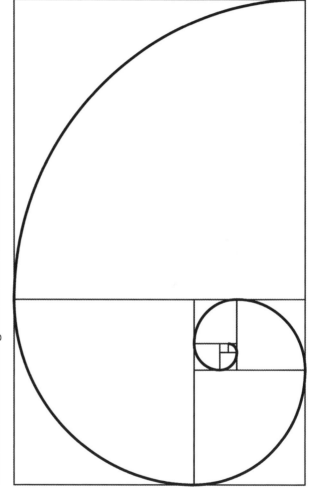

#137

Name as many things as you can that have got an eye but cannot see.

#138

What's the single most important skill (or characteristic) anyone should learn?

#139

What's your biggest worry right now? You don't have to share it with anyone, just have a think. Is there anything or anyone that could help with it?

#140

A ball was thrown as hard as possible. It didn't hit anything. There was nothing attached to it and no one else caught it or threw it and yet it came back to the thrower. How?

#141

Who do you most want to impress? Why them?

#142

Recently, Paul Allan (a teacher from Northamptonshire) won the British National Scrabble Championships against a Scrabble consultant. Encouragingly, you don't have to know obscure words to win at Scrabble – 'UGH' and 'YEAH' were two of the words he used. His winning word, however, was slightly more obscure: BANDURA – a Ukrainian stringed instrument.

Pick seven letters at random (choose any seven pages in this book and count 12 letters along each time).

What's the most interesting word you can come up with, just using your brain?

#143

As well as being a girl's name, the word 'grace' is a really powerful thing. It's about doing something amazing for someone who really doesn't deserve it at all; in fact they deserve the opposite. It's all about forgiveness when you least deserve it and it's powerful.

Think of someone – someone you find quite unlikeable – and decide today how you can do something to help them.

#144

Rock-Paper-Scissors can be used as a way of remembering angles (acute beats straight line and so on). Battleships is a good way of practising co-ordinates. How could noughts and crosses (or tic-tac-toe) be used to help you learn something?

#145 List •

eight phrases

we all should say *a lot less*.

#146

We can't see the wind, but we know it's there by feeling it and seeing the effect that it has. List as many things as you can that you can't see but you know are there ...

#147

Sometimes big numbers aren't clear until you give them a real-world value. If someone said they were going to run 384,400 km over the course of the next couple of years it might not mean much to you, but if they said they were going to run the distance to the moon, you'd have a better idea of whether they could do it or not.

Come up with real-world values for as many number measurements as you can (temperature, distance, age, time, weight, and so on)[1].

#148

Order these three creatures in order of danger to humans.

#149

In the lobby of Google's HQ in California (the Googleplex) they have a projection of all the live Google search queries that are being searched at that moment across the world. What do you think the trending topics would be today?

---

1 If you use Google Chrome, you might like to take a look at this extension, which attempts to make sense of numbers on the web by attaching a human value to them: <http://www.dictionaryofnumbers.com/>.

#150

Some people say, 'Things always happen for a reason.' What do you think?

#151

What makes an outstanding lesson?[1]

#152

In the same way that people say, 'I'm tone deaf' or, 'I haven't got an ear for music', do you think some people have no eye for art, no nose for perfume or no taste buds for pea soup?

#153

Before this piece of paper was folded over once it was a capital letter. It wasn't the letter L – that would be too easy. Which letter was it?

#154

Your head teacher asks you, 'Do you like my new haircut?' and, if you're being honest, you think it looks like a cat is balancing on her head. You have two seconds to make a decision – which is more important, honesty or politeness?

---

1 You can watch a little video with some of the things that we think make an outstanding teacher here: <http://www.sparkyteaching.com/creative/now-thats-what-i-call-outstanding/>.

#155

What was the last thing you sacrificed for someone else?

#156

What makes someone an artist? Are YOU an artist?

#157

How much of an effect does the boss of a company, the principal of a school or a sports coach have on success? Why?

#158

You probably know your 11 times table. It's fairly easy when you are multiplying by single digits. But try this little trick for multiplying two-digit numbers by 11. Add the two digits together. Then write the total in the middle of them to get the answer.

Does this always work?

#159

Let's play Boy-Girl-Fruit-Flower. Can you think of a boy's name, girl's name, fruit (or vegetable) and flower for every letter of the alphabet? Be brave and go without Google!

♂	♀	↺	✿

#160

What are the three 'NEVER's of your life?

#161

When you're most happy, what is it that you are doing?

#162

Sometimes giving yourself rules for writing forces you to come up with more interesting ideas. A lipogram is a piece of writing that has a rule. For instance, it might not contain the letter 'e' or the only vowel it contains is 'o'. Have a go at this. Try writing a mystery story in 100 words, the start to your favourite story only using words of one-syllable or a poem about cats without using the letter 'a'.

#163

Complete the line graph.

LINE GRAPH TO SHOW HOW THE AUTHOR, _____ , BUILDS TENSION
IN THEIR BOOK, _____.

READER TENSION

KEY EVENTS IN THE STORY

#164

How can you trust something or someone you can't see?

#165

You have a time machine. Here are some facts about it:

- – It's the size of a wardrobe.
- – It's a lot slower than you'd expect and travels shorter distances than Doctor Who's Tardis (minutes and hours, rather than hundreds of years).
- – It only takes you forwards in time, never backwards.

Can you figure out what is being described here?

#166

Complete the Venn diagram.

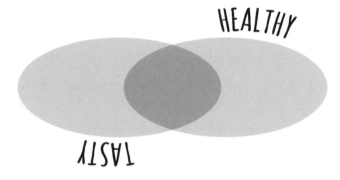

#167

What one thing are you most grateful for?

#168

You have one wish, but you can't wish for something for yourself. What would you wish for?

#165

WILL BOOKS EVER BECOME EXTINCT?

#170

Without moving from where you are, frame something that
is amazing.

#171

Messages from the world of advertising and television seem to tell us that people have to look a certain way. It's not surprising that many young people grow up insecure about their body image. In real life, nobody looks like the airbrushed ads in magazines.

In a world of such messages, how could your school help those who feel self-conscious and fed up with the way they look?

#172

'To get respect you have to earn it. Teachers shouldn't just get the respect of pupils.' 'Respect comes with age. You should respect older people.'

What do you think?

#173

If you work for Google, you used to be given 20% of your time to work on your own projects. Google's email application, Gmail, began life as someone's 20% project.

What would you do with one day a week if your school gave you 20% time too?[1]

---

1 Teachers, this question was inspired by a section in Zoë Elder's *Full On Learning: Involve Me and I'll Understand* (Crown House, 2012). You really ought to read it.

#174

Sister Helen P. Mrosla was a nun who taught for over 35 years. Years ago she gave her class the following assignment. She sent them home with a blank piece of paper and asked them to write their own name at the top and their classmates' names down the side. Next to each name, they were asked to write down the thing they most liked about that person. After collecting in her class's responses, Sister Helen prepared a sheet for each person with all the positive comments about them collected together.

To cut a long story short, years later she was asked to attend the funeral of one of her students who had been killed in Vietnam, Mark Eklund. After the service, Mark's mother approached Sister Helen and told her that amongst Mark's personal belongings brought back from Vietnam was a piece of paper that had been taped together many times and was falling apart. It was Mark's piece of paper with all his classmates' comments on.

Sister Helen sat with Mark's classmates at the funeral, and one by one they told her how much they had appreciated her little assignment. One had kept their piece of paper in the top drawer of their desk, another had put theirs in their wedding album and someone else reached into their pocket and pulled theirs out.

Different people get different things from this story, but why not try carrying out Sister Helen's assignment yourselves?[1] You'll get much more from it than from just reading what happened.

---

1 Teachers who care about their students' characters as well as their test scores could do a lot worse than read Sister Helen's account in her own words: <http://www.educationworld.com/a_lesson/lesson/lesson012.shtml>.

NAME	WHAT I MOST APPRECIATE

#175

Glen James, a homeless man in Boston (US), found a bag containing $42,000. Despite his need, he did the right thing and handed the lost bag in. A complete stranger heard about his honesty and started up an online fund for Mr James. At the time of writing, that fund has now reached $110,000 and the man who started it is going to meet Mr James to give him the money.

Being honest won't always get you $110,000 (in fact, often it will make you worse off and sometimes might even get you into trouble), but in what other ways does it pay to be truthful?

#176

How long have you been on this planet for? Use four different units of measurement to answer this question and, if you really want a challenge, make one of those units something non-standard (e.g. the time it takes to cook an omelette).

#177

Your boss has told you that you will be fired unless you can answer his question correctly. It's, 'Will you still be working for me at the end of today?' He will only accept a yes or no answer. If you get the wrong answer or if you don't answer at all you lose your job.

What should you say to be guaranteed your job at the end of the day?

#178

Some people say that we have to be sad sometimes to feel happiness at other times. What do you think? Is darkness needed to show what light is?

#179

What's your personal motto? (If you don't have one, make one up!)

#180

Name three foods that are easy to ruin and three foods that you could do pretty much anything to and they would still taste amazing.

#181

Do we all see colours the same or differently?

Ashrith, Y4, Rickmansworth Park JMI School, Herts

#182

Tomorrow you are going to be taught by someone new. Apart from your name, what one piece of information do you want them to know about you?

#183

In Class 6W, George and Nia are joint winners of the Spelling Challenge. The prize is £100. Being slightly mischievous, their teacher splits them into separate rooms where they can't talk to each other. He then visits each one in turn and gives them some options.

'I'm going to speak to you both individually and you can either choose to share the money or take it. Those are your options – Share or Take – nothing else. If you both say Share, I'll award you £50 each. If you both say Take, neither of you will get any money and I'll use it to buy really hard maths tests for the class. If one of you says Share and the other one says Take, the Taker will get all of the £100.'[1]

Remember, George and Nia are in separate rooms and can't communicate with each other. Apart from 'Go to a different school where the teachers are less annoying', what would you advise them to do and why?

---

1 This little challenge is a variation of something called The Prisoner's Dilemma, which has been used by economists to explain human behaviour and economic theory and by TV show hosts to liven up quiz shows.

#184

Using only the numbers on the cards, how close can you get to the target number?

TARGET NUMBER:

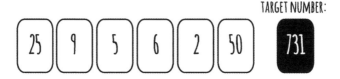

25 9 5 6 2 50 731

#185

Would you rather play badly and win the game or play with style and lose? Can you apply this idea to life as well as sport?

#186

Come up with some ingenious ways to remember this Wi-Fi password: BHWR1POD

#187

Can we really describe water as fresh? Isn't it the same water as centuries ago, just having gone round the water cycle a few times? In fact, when you think about it, is anything actually new?

#188

Are you an animal?

#189

As well as being one of the weirdest songs ever, Ylvis' YouTube hit 'The Fox' is clearly not true. Not the bit about foxes – we all know they go 'ring-ding-ding' – it's the other animal noises that aren't true. The sound an animal makes depends on what language you speak. In Spanish, dogs go 'guan, guan' and in Japanese cats go 'nyah, nyah'.[1]

Can you write more onomatopoeic versions of farmyard noises that are a better fit to the animals' sounds?

#190

Your teacher has said you can escape homework this week only if you can demonstrate a multiplication that makes one million. There's one problem. She's given you a calculator where the zero button isn't working. The clock is ticking. Will you get out of homework or not?

#191

Someone said recently that when they need to come up with ideas, they do lots of research and fill their mind with images and information about the subject. Then they do something completely unrelated to work. It's during this time, when they're not concentrating on it, that they find most of their ideas arrive.

How could you use this method in class?

---

1 For more fascinating international animal noises, see here: <http://www.esl-languages.com/en/animal-sounds.htm>.

#192

A Tom Swiftie is a special way of playing with words. The name comes from the Tom Swift series of books, in which the author tended to avoid the word 'said'. Tom Swifties also include an adverb on the end that makes a play on words. Can you explain the jokes here? (Look at the last word very closely ...)

'I'm not going outside in this rain,' Tom remarked drily.

'I won't be cleaning alligator's teeth ever again,' Tom sighed offhandedly.

'Now, let me prop my painting up ... ' said Tom easily.

Once you can see what's going on, have a go at some Tom Swifties of your own. Here are some for starters:

_____ Tom croaked.

_____ muttered Tom crabbily.

_____ yelled Tom alarmingly.

_____ Tom noted.

_____ Tom pointed out.

#193

FOR SALE   SPARKY HOMES

Four-bedroomed, fully-insulated, detached house in remote location.

Every window in the house (front, back and sides) is South facing.

There's nothing too unusual about sentence one, but how is the second sentence possible?

#19

100

#195

Design an experiment to test how selfless people in your school are.

#196

A letter arrived. An old lady picked it up. It read 'I will get you back some day!' Who do you think wrote it and why?

P6b, Cornbank St James School, Penicuik

#197

Is it possible to choose what happens in your dreams?

#198

What have you done today (or will you do) to make you feel proud?

#199

Come up with five useful strategies to use when you're asked a question you don't know the answer to.

#200

What job would you enjoy so much, no amount of money could make you give it up?

Go for it!

#201

Someone recently answered a question on wishes by saying, 'I'd wish for infinite wishes.' But can you foresee any problems with having an infinite number of wishes or a never-ending pot of money? What would happen in the first hour? What would happen in the weeks and months that followed?

#202

What are your four best tips for someone who wants to be a teacher?

#203

If A=1% B=2% C=3% and so on, what are each of these words worth?

MONEY

FAME

FRIENDS

HARD WORK

ATTITUDE

{ WHETHER YOU THINK YOU CAN OR THINK YOU CAN'T – YOU'RE RIGHT. } HENRY FORD
U.S. Industrialist

#204

{ BUT THE IDEA OF THE NEST IN THE BIRD'S MIND? WHERE DOES IT COME FROM? } JOSEPH JOUBERT
Writer

Have you ever seen birds stamping the ground? It's to get worms to come to the surface. But where did they get the idea to do that from? How did the first bird to do that pass on the information to the next generation?

#205

You are in charge of deciding pay scales. Put these jobs in order of who you think should be paid the most. Discuss why you've chosen this order:

> NURSE
>
> RSPCA OFFICER
>
> SCULPTOR
>
> FOOTBALLER
>
> WEB DESIGNER
>
> POP SINGER

An extension question: in real life, why are people who save lives (like firefighters and nurses) paid so much less than footballers or celebrities?

#206

Hypothetical questions are questions that get you to use your imagination in the answer. They usually begin with words like 'What if', 'How might' or, occasionally, 'Here's a hypothetical question for you'.

Write three questions beginning with the words 'What if ... '

For each question, write a follow-up question beginning with the word 'Would ... ' e.g. What if pigs could fly? Would they still be kept as farm animals?

#207

How many gifts will your true love have given to you by the end of the song 'The Twelve Days of Christmas'?* If you work this out correctly, it makes a pretty interesting answer! Why?

*Remember, most of the gifts are repeated several times (on Day Two, you'll get three gifts – two turtle doves plus another partridge in a pear tree to add to the one you got on Day One, and so on!)

#208

If you go into the country, miles away from anywhere, and stare up at the sky on a clear night, you'll see more stars than you ever imagined were there. These stars haven't just appeared. They're out there every night (and every day, if you think about it) – it's just that man-made light pollution (during the night) and the sun (during the day) means we don't see them. It's only when we take these things away that we can really stop and stare.

Take some things away (any distractions or sounds) and take time to really look at something. What can you spot that you never knew was there?

#209

Can you fill in this crossword?

To challenge yourself, try limiting your
answers to just adjectives or
only words beginning with
a certain letter.

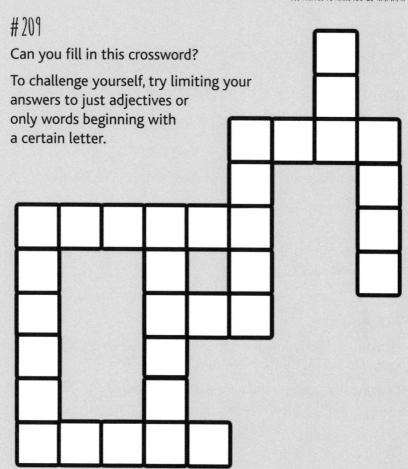

#210

Your teacher will retire in a world that you run. Should they be worried?

#211

If you woke up tomorrow with no fear, what would you do first?

#212

Can you connect yourself with someone famous in no more than five steps?

#213

What's the difference between selfish and selfless? How can you be more selfless today?[1]

#214

Your phone rings.

'Hi there,' a slightly wooden voice on the other end says. 'I just wanted to say my nose is really long.'

It's Pinocchio. Think carefully. Is he telling the truth?

---

1 For selflessness in action, watch this: <http://www.youtube.com/watch?v=0Ejh_hb15Fc&app=desktop>. The best thing about this is that it didn't come from an adult.

#215

'Do or do not. There is no try.'

Master Yoda, *Star Wars*

Can you what he means explain?

#216

We read about a book recently where, in the margins of the pages, there are little notes to and from two of the readers of the story (these are made up by the author). So there is a story happening between the readers alongside the story that they're supposed to be reading. All of which, you are reading too! If you dare, try doing something similar in class! Use sticky notes to write the readers' messages on and have them react to the story as they read it. Maybe one is enjoying the story and the other isn't.

#217 DO YOUR BEST TO EXPLAIN THE MEANINGS OF INFINITY & ETERNITY.

#218

What would happen in a world without trees?

Mr Woodburn's Class, Year 4, Milnthorpe Primary School, Cumbria

#219

What do the clouds see?[1]

Tiffany, Cedar Class, Liberty Primary School, Merton

---

1 This question is so descriptive, try writing a poem based on the idea of clouds looking down on the world. There's a lot of potential in that idea.

#220

If you look up in the sky on a sunny day,
it's sometimes fun to spot shapes that the clouds make –
a pig on a Harley Davidson or your dad with a wig on.

How long, though, does it take for a cumulus cloud
(fluffy, looks like cotton wool) to disperse?

The best way to answer this is to estimate
the time you think and then, on a sunny
day, choose a cloud and watch it until
it breaks up. It's an exercise in
stopping still and actually
looking at something that
you probably usually only
look at for a couple of
seconds.

You may be surprised by the answer.

#221

You're now part of Sparky Teaching's Worldwide Game of Tag. Here are the rules:

1. Each person who is 'it' is only allowed to tag one person a day. The game only began today and you're the first person to be tagged.

2. When someone is tagged, they are 'it' too. So tomorrow there'll be two people who will go out and tag one new person each. The following day there will be four people and so on.

How long until there's no one left in the world to tag?

It will be a lot more interesting to make a prediction first, before you try to work it out.

222

What's the longest word you can make from these letters?

How do you tend to do this sort of activity? What strategies do you use?

223

The best activities make you lose track of time. Which activities have that effect on you?

224

Does a film spoil the book?

225

Many famous people are also 'brands' nowadays, having designed their own logo that they put on everything from baseball caps to perfume.[1] Think carefully about what would sum YOU up. What would your logo look like?

226

Will the world ever be completely peaceful or are disagreements and wars inevitable?

---

1 Design company four23 made a video showing how they designed logos for Olympic athletes Christine Ohuruogu and Mo Farah. You can watch it here: <https://vimeo.com/73934073>. It's interesting to see how (and why) they came up with both logos to suit the athletes.

#227

Look closely at these beautifully designed ampersands:

Can you work out why we use this symbol to represent 'and'?

CLUE: You are looking for a hidden word. It is very short, Latin and you might need the help of Google to find out what it means! Once you spot it, you'll realise why people used to write etcetera as &c.

#228

Apparently, 99% of the human body is made up of oxygen, carbon, hydrogen, nitrogen, calcium and phosphorus. Does that mean we're just a load of chemicals then?

#229

Someone is interested in finding out how heavy their head is. Without doing themselves an injury[1], what's the most accurate way of weighing it?

#230

An exercise in seeing things from others' points of view. Come up with five convincing reasons to argue that you should be given a lot more homework.

---

1 This bit is quite important.

#231

In a world where loud people often get heard, what are the positives in being quiet?

#232

If your parents ruled the world, what changes would everyone notice?

#233

'Websites shouldn't allow people to post anonymously and should keep a record of every comment or photo that is uploaded. That way people would think twice before posting inappropriate or hurtful stuff.'

Discuss!

#234

Using only the digits 1-9 (keeping them in this order) and using either + or − symbols, how many ways can you find of making 100?

#235

You are in the middle of a lesson and stuck. You just can't get past the question you are on. Without speaking to your teacher, what strategies can you use for unsticking yourself?

#236

Good Friday is the name of the day when Jesus died. What's good about someone dying?

#237

Choose three words from this list that you think would make the best learner:

DECISIVE   YOUNG   OLD   RISKY   CONVENTIONAL
UNCONVENTIONAL   VARIABLE   CONSTANT   CERTAIN

#238

The most creative people say they get ideas from anywhere. How could a letter addressed to the wrong person inspire you today?

#239

'Who is the teacher here? You or me?'
'This is your own time you're wasting ... '
'That bell's for me, not for you!'
'Has anyone seen the whiteboard pen?'

What well-worn catchphrases does your teacher have? Invent some new ones for them.

#240

You're guaranteed the answer to one question, but you're not allowed to share the answer with anyone else. Ever. What do you want to ask?

241

Is the future like a map that we just can't see or like a map that hasn't been drawn yet?

There are some interesting follow-up questions to this one ...

- — If our lives are part of a bigger plan, who drew it?
- — If you had the opportunity to see your map, would you want to see it?
- — Is there anything you can do to change your map?
- — How much does where you go in life depend on where you've come from?

LET'S HEAR IT FOR

THE FOOD
PIONEERS!

We hear a lot about PIONEER EXPLORERS going to places for the first time, often suffering greatly and some giving their lives in the process.

The PIONEERS OF MEDICINE did a similar thing. Some people suffered as treatments were tried out to see if they worked.

As a SLIGHTLY SILLY EXAMPLE of this, question number 242 is about

THE PIONEERS OF FOOD!

BRAVE MEN AND WOMEN
VENTURING INTO THE CULINARY UNKNOWN
WITH ONLY THEIR TASTEBUDS FOR COMPANY.

Someone somewhere decided to eat THE BULB OF A PLANT for the first time and was probably VERY ILL. Maybe they experimented a few times and got several more STOMACH ACHES until they found one that didn't make them feel quite so unwell. In time, they decided it tasted nice fried and lo, THE ONION was discovered! Think of the suffering involved in the discovery of CHILLI PEPPERS too...

#242 WHICH OTHER PIONEERS OF FOOD SHOULD WE TIP OUR HATS TO?

243

Try playing this game with a partner. You have to count out loud to 20. Each player in turn has to say either one, two or three consecutive numbers. The loser is the player who ends up saying the word 'twenty.' Play the game a few times. Is there a way to make sure you win?

244

What is true strength? Try to explain what you mean.

245

The government has written to your head teacher saying they have to get rid of one subject based on how unimportant it is. Which one should go? Why?

Your head teacher has misread the letter. It actually says that they have to get rid of ALL subjects and keep only one, based on how important it is. Which one should stay? Why?

246

Invent a powerful class motto that sums you up.

247

If someone spent a day inside your mind, how would they be feeling by the end of it? Why?

#248

'Maybe if everything was beautiful, nothing would be.'

Dean Koontz, author

What do you think this means? Do you agree?

#249

h n! We've just nticed that the letter between I and P isn't wrking n ur cmputer keybard. What shuld these wrds be?

utdr　　bnxius　　ctpus　　nlker　　ppsitin　　vd　　cckat　　cane　　ccasinal

#250

In the 1960s, David Ogilvy (a man who worked in advertising) was walking down the street and came across a homeless man with a sign saying, 'I am blind'. The cup in front of the man was empty. Ogilvy took a pen and changed the wording on the man's sign to, 'It is Spring. I am blind.' The man was given more money.

Why did the change in wording make a difference? Can you learn any lessons from this?[1]

#251

What have you done today to harm our planet?

What can you do differently tomorrow to charm our planet?

---

1 As a follow-up to this discussion, you might want to have a look at <http://homelesssigns.tumblr.com/>, where graphic designers replaced handwritten signs for typographic efforts in a bid to raise awareness about the homeless (not to increase giving). Each homeless person was paid for their old sign and many were helped to find housing and work in the area. Do you think this is a good way to raise awareness or just a stunt?

#252

Grab a pen and a piece of paper. Now start making a number triangle like this ...

Start off with a 1 at the top and then write the total of each pair of digits underneath them in a new layer. Keep adding as many layers as you can. This is called Pascal's triangle (named after the man who invented it, French mathematician Blaise Pascal) and it's great for spotting patterns.

HOW MANY LAYERS DID YOU GET TO? WHICH PATTERNS CAN YOU SPOT!

253

A teacher[1] once walked into an exam room and announced: 'Here is the exam. Write your own questions. Write your own answers. Harder questions and better answers get more points.'

Have a go at this!

254

255

If the minute hand is on top of the hour hand, what time could it be?

(There's more than one answer to this!)

256

'Doing your best is more important than being the best.'

Is that really true?

---

1 The teacher was Tyler Cowen, the US economist, academic and writer. He said that it was the question where he thought he learned most about his students. <http://blog.sethroberts.net/2012/08/09/tyler-cowens-unusual-final-exam/>.

#257

MURPHY'S LAW
OF THE CLASSROOM

Murphy's Law says that 'if something can go wrong, it probably will'. Here are some examples of Murphy's Laws:

THE LAW OF TOAST
When you drop a piece of toast on the floor, it will always land buttery side down, making a massive greasy mess on your carpet.

THE LAW OF MESSY HANDS
The minute you start getting your hands dirty, your nose will start to itch.

Can you come up with some Murphy's Laws for your classroom?

For example:

THE LAW OF THE CLASSROOM CLOCK
When it's free time the minute hand speeds up; when it's a lesson on fractions it moves extremely slowly.

Here are some titles to get you started:

- THE LAW OF THE PE KIT
- THE LAW OF THE SCHOOL TRIP
- THE LAW OF THE MATHS TEST
- THE LAW OF RAIN

121

258

In the winter of 2012, a New York Police Department officer saw a homeless man sitting in the cold with bare feet. He went into a nearby shop, bought some new boots with his own money and gave them to the homeless man. He didn't tell anyone else, but (unbeknownst to him) someone photographed him in the act of giving the boots.

The NYPD officer was simply caught being kind.

Think of ways you can help someone else today on the quiet.

There's a follow-up to this story ...

The photo of the NYPD officer went viral on the Internet and his little act of quiet kindness soon became known worldwide. About a week later, some reporters tried to contact the homeless man to talk to him about what had happened, but when they caught up with him he was still barefoot. He explained that the boots were too expensive so he'd hidden them somewhere to prevent himself from getting beaten up by someone who'd want to steal them. You can read the rest of the story here:

<http://www.theguardian.com/commentisfree/2012/dec/04/homeless-man-nypd-cop-boots>

There are lots of questions that could be asked about these events (about newspapers, things going viral, how best to help a homeless person in a New York winter), but here is the one we decided on:

Even though things didn't turn out the way the NYPD officer intended and the man still has cold feet, what are the positives (if any) in the story?

#259

On 14 October 2012, just after 12 noon (US time), a 43-year-old man stood on his step and looked out at the world. It was a clear day and he could see for miles. But this wasn't some ordinary man taking a look at the world outside his house. His name was Felix Baumgartner and his step was on a balloon, 23 miles above planet Earth on the edge of space. No doubt he took a very deep breath and then he jumped.

If that was you, what could motivate you to step off?[1]

#260

Should children be able to watch whatever film certificate their parents allow?

#261

Some post was recently delivered to a house in Winchester. When Keith and Sue Webb went to open their parcel, it contained an oil painting of an old lady with a hooked nose. Although it was addressed to Mr Webb, there was no note and they had no idea where the painting had been sent from. The painting was so strange, Mrs Webb told her husband to keep it in the garage.

Come up with a possible story to explain this mystery.

---

1 If you don't have the daredevil gene, you might prefer to skydive to Google Earth instead. This only works on Google Chrome browsers: <http://mapdive.weareinstrument.com/>.

sparky teaching

These great posters were designed (and written) by Pete Jones' Year 8 students at Les Quennevais School as part of their Pebble (PBL) project. Part of their inspiration was our 'This Is Not A Classroom' poster: <www.sparkyteaching.com/resources/motivational/messagesthatmatter.php>. Pete's blog is a mine of creative ideas: <deeplearning.edublogs.org/>.

IN THIS CLASSROOM,
WE ARE THE PEOPLE THAT LIVE TO SUCCEED AND LOVE TO ACHIEVE,
WE HAVE RESPECT,
WE LISTEN AND SUPPORT ALL OUR FRIENDS,
THIS IS WHERE OUR MOTIVATION, DETERMINATION AND CONCENTRATION NEVER ENDS.
WE DON'T KNOW WHAT THE FUTURE WILL BRING,
SO ALL WE CAN DO IS PREPARE.
WE WILL WORK AT OUR BEST,
EVEN IF THAT'S NOT BETTER THAN THE REST.
THIS IS OUR OPPORTUNITY TO LET OUR SKILLS ENLARGE,
'COS ONE DAY OUR WORK WILL PAY OFF AND WE'LL BE IN CHARGE.
SOME PEOPLE ARE GREAT,
THEY SEE LIGHT BULBS 'DING',
SKILLS AND GREAT THINGS ARE WHAT LEARNING WILL BRING.
ANYONE FROM ANYWHERE CAN LEARN 'LIKE A PRO',
BUT SOME JUST GIVE UP AND DON'T WANNA KNOW.
EVEN THE BRIGHTEST MINDS IN THE SCHOOL,
COULD ACT FOOLISH,
SEEM NOT CLEVER AT ALL.
TO BECOME THE BEST YOU CAN BE,
YOU NEED THE PATIENCE AND PRACTISE,
AND THE HARD WORK TO PROGRESS,
BUT LIFE ISN'T JUST ABOUT GETTING GOOD RESULTS OR BEATING THE OTHERS,
IT'S ABOUT PREPARING,

IMPROVING,

ADAPTING,

BELIEVING.

this is not a classroom.
it might look like one
but

this is our base of operation.
this is a place where we
accept challenges and embrace
them.

we learn from our teams

criticism.
become creative and independent
these two skills lead up to

bravery.
respect other people and they will
respect you back.
a positive attitude is a key to open doors
giving you the best opportunity

of a lifetime.
taking risks will boost your confidence

these are the skills you will

learn about in pebble.
if you learn these skills you will
have a great

future.

262

When is a classroom not a classroom?

sparky teaching

263

I DON'T MIND IF I HAVE TO SIT ON THE FLOOR AT SCHOOL.

~

ALL I WANT IS EDUCATION. AND I'M AFRAID OF NO ONE.

MALALA YOUSAFZAI

You would expect to be able to travel to and from school safely, but in October 2012, Malala Yousafzai – a school pupil from Pakistan – was trying to do just that when she was shot. She was 14 years old. Many believe she was attacked because of the stand she took on education for all – even before this event she was an inspiration to many. Her subsequent recovery and attitude has since been an inspiration to many more. Thankfully, she was treated in hospital and has made good progress recovering in Birmingham. If you've never heard of her, look her up – you'll be inspired.

Every day, all over the world, children just like Malala take extraordinary risks to go to school – in war zones or even walking across mountains.[1] The classrooms that await some of these children aren't the sort of carpeted, warm, iPad-containing classrooms some of you enjoy – in fact there is a photo out there of a collection of students sitting on the ground underneath a motorway flyover – but still these children walk miles to make the journey every day.

Is there a difference in attitude towards education between the children in your country and those in these places? If so, why do you think this is? If not, what's the same?

---

1 Here is an amazing collection of photos of the journeys some students take around the world to get to school: <http://www.telegraph.co.uk/travel/picturegalleries/9930291/Extreme-school-run-children-going-to-great-lengths-in-order-to-get-to-school.html>.

264

Since the Internet, have we become more or less clever?

265

These shapes have been made by putting letters on top of each other. They are all three-letter words.

A B C D E F G H I J K L M N O P Q R S T U V W X Y Z

What are the words?

266

'Life's most persistent and urgent question is: What are you doing for others?'

Martin Luther King

What are you doing for other people?

As a follow-up, you could think about whether there are any questions that are more persistent and urgent.

267

Who do you look at and think: 'What a great person, I'd really like to be like them'? And why do you admire them?

268

This is called an ambigram. Have a go at writing an ambigram of your first name.

269

If there was a device that showed exactly when you would die, would you want to know?

P7, St Margaret's Primary, Cowie

270

Is not speaking out against something the same as being for it?

271

Some of the most creative people, whether they are animators, scientists or software designers, don't just solve problems. They go looking for them.

Two such people were working on a problem, trying to put the results of library book searches into a reasonable order. Instead of being happy with solving that problem for libraries, they then thought of a bigger problem – putting the results of Internet searches into order. They worked hard on applying the first answer to the second problem and now Google is the most used search engine in the world.

What problems can you identify in your school? In the world?

Choose one and come up with as many solutions to it as possible. If you were investing in one of these solutions, which would you choose?

#272

Why on t ?

THIS IS A NOTE FOR YOU – THE READER!

In films and TV, the Fourth Wall is the imaginary wall between the actors and the audience. It gets broken when someone talks to the audience directly. Like we're doing with you now.

Take an extract from a book or play that you've been studying and have a go at getting one of the characters to address the reader/audience directly. What happens next?

#273

On 3 October 2013, a piece of street art appeared on a wall in New York. It wasn't long before people started noticing it and it was confirmed as being painted by the artist Banksy, whose works now sell for incredible amounts of money. A day later it was painted over (probably by the authorities), but people still turned up to take photos of the grey, painted-over wall where it was.

Was Banksy's work art? Graffiti? Both? Neither?

Was the painted-over wall worth taking a photo of?

What if you found out Banksy had painted over it himself in a piece he called *Life is Like a New York Wall?* Would it be art then?

#274

A man looks out of the window, sees a shadowy shape and tells his wife that he knows the dog has escaped outside. They step into the garden, but closer inspection reveals that the shape is just a garden sack. All his worry disappears.

Then, just as they're about to go inside, his wife sees a familiar furry figure sprinting merrily off down the road. The dog *has* escaped, but the reason they know this is not because of that shadowy shape the man saw.

When he looked out of the window and said what he said, even though it was based on false information, can it still be said to be true?

#275

'Without money we'd all be rich.'

What does this mean?

#276

Someone once said,

'Sentences end with full stops. Stories do not.'[1]

What do you think he meant?

#277

How long would it take you to reach space if cars could drive upwards?[2]

First have a guess, then do some research. You might be surprised at the answer.

#278

'School uniforms teach you to be the same as everyone else.'

Discuss!

#279

What do you think motivates your teacher to keep coming into school every day and teaching you? Are they deluded?

Now ask them what their motivation is.[3]

---

1 Interestingly, it was Harold Rosen, the father of children's poet, author, teachers' friend and bear-hunter Michael Rosen.

2 Assuming that the speed limit is 60mph on a single-lane skyway.

3 A clue: it's not for the money.

280

Let's build a metaphorical brain! If you had to make one completely out of everyday objects, what would you choose to represent the different tasks your brain does?

281

Sometimes teachers take something unusual or interesting and use it to teach a subject. For example, using cartoons to start a history lesson, meerkats in a lesson on fractions or hip-hop music to learn about poetry. What examples have you experienced? Why do teachers do this?

282

Is street dancing a sport? In fact, while you're at it, what is a sport?

283

Should rich people be forced to give more to charity than people who have less?

284

**KEEP OUT
NO SKATEBOARDING
ALLOWED**

Can you punctuate this sign so it means two opposite things?

#285

'WHATEVER IS

TRUE
NOBLE
RIGHT
PURE
LOVELY
ADMIRABLE

if anything is **EXCELLENT** or **PRAISEWORTHY ...**

THINK ABOUT THESE THINGS.'

Philippians 4:8
THE BIBLE

How does what you think about affect who you are?

#286

What's one thing that most people find fairly easy, but you've always found a bit tricky?

287

Every day on the website we post a new question to make your class go Hmmm. On one occasion we didn't feel it was suitable.

On 14 December, 2012 in Newtown, Connecticut, 20 children and 6 adults lost their lives in a shooting at an elementary school. On 15 December it just didn't seem appropriate to ask a big question. Instead we showed this message. When it came to putting the book together it seemed important to include it:

. . . .

Today, there's no question.

Instead, spend the time you would have spent answering to think about or pray for anyone who may be grieving at this time.

And maybe, just take a moment to appreciate all the special people in your life. Sometimes it's important just to say thank you.

. . . .

288

Sometimes things are noticeable by their absence. What's the most insignificant thing you can think of that would be really noticeable if it wasn't there?

289

A local residential home. The noticeboard in the Post Office. A blog. A dog.

Find an audience for your writing that you never knew existed.

290

Write two lists: one of things that technology has replaced and the other of things that technology will never replace. Is it true to say the things in your second list are more important than the things in the first? Why is technology unable to replace the things in your second list?

291

Does listening to music help you concentrate? If so, can you come up with a playlist for being creative?

#292

A contagious challenge: can you make the person who read this question to you smile?

If you're reading it to yourself on a bus, make yourself laugh (a proper belly laugh).[1]

#293

If you want to be the sort of person who could tell a policeman exactly what the burglar looked like or the number plate of the van that drove off, how could you improve the speed of your visual memory?

#294

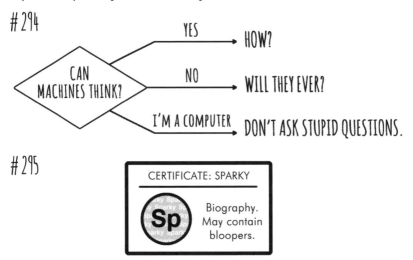

CAN MACHINES THINK?

YES → HOW?

NO → WILL THEY EVER?

I'M A COMPUTER → DON'T ASK STUPID QUESTIONS.

#295

CERTIFICATE: SPARKY

Sp

Biography. May contain bloopers.

In a film of your life so far, what would feature in the out-takes?

#296

Name 10 body parts which are spelt with three letters.

---

1 You get extra points if, by doing this, you make the old lady opposite you start laughing too. Watch you don't get in trouble for causing too much hilarity in a public place.

UNDERSTAND.
CHANGE.
THINK.
FEEL.
ACT.

#297

RATE THESE WORDS IN ORDER OF HOW IMPORTANT THEY ARE
FOR YOUR TEACHER TO MAKE YOU DO IN LESSONS.
WHY HAVE YOU CHOSEN THIS ORDER?

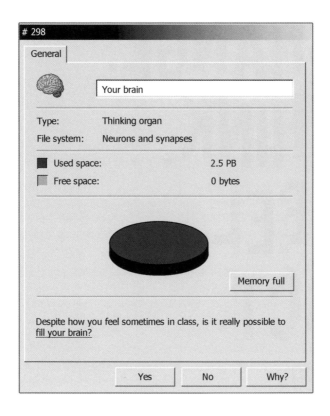

 # 298

General

Your brain

Type:	Thinking organ
File system:	Neurons and synapses

■ Used space: 2.5 PB

□ Free space: 0 bytes

Memory full

Despite how you feel sometimes in class, is it really possible to fill your brain?

Yes	No	Why?

#299

What's something you do differently to most people? What makes you one in seven billion?

#300

Why do we have to learn?
Maple Tree Class, Tirlebrook Primary School, Gloucs

#301

'Every child is an artist. The problem is how to remain an artist once he grows up.'
Pablo Picasso

There's a lot of truth in that quote. Ask a group of adults to draw a cow with three legs and a lot more of them will say, 'I'm no good at drawing!' than if you asked the same number of children.

How do you plan to stay creative as you grow older?

#302

Which cartoon character would make the best friend? Why?

#303

How much information about yourself is it okay to share online?

#304

On 5 September 1977, the Voyager I space probe was launched into space. At the time of writing (36 years later) it's still going! One of the most fascinating things about Voyager I is that it only has about 68kb of memory on board. A digital photo of Voyager I takes up over twenty times more memory!

On Voyager I is a golden phonograph record with sounds and images to show what Earth and its inhabitants are like. They were chosen in case the probe bumped into any extra-terrestrial life forms along the way. It includes a message from the US president at the time, Jimmy Carter: 'This is a present from a small, distant world, a token of our sounds, our science, our images, our music, our thoughts and our feelings. We are attempting to survive our time so we may live into yours.'

What sounds, images, words and music would you include to sum up this incredible planet we live on?

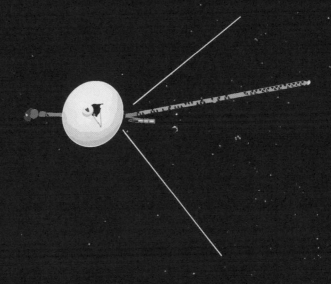

#305

Since Voyager I was launched, it's been travelling at a speed of 1.4 million km per day. In 2012 it was announced that it is still continuing on its way out of our solar system. One day it will run out of fuel (probably 2020), but what would happen if it kept on going?

What do you think is beyond the universe?

#306

Why do things have to die?

#307

Is there life after death?

#308

'Tests are pointless. They're just for the teachers. Children don't really benefit from them. They're just stressful things that reward those students who have good memories, not those that are actually skilled at something. In fact, they're better at testing what you don't know than what you do.'

Discuss!

#309

Your job is to market a noise vacuum called Pure Quiet. It sucks up noise. Name five good things about quietness and five places your vacuum could be used to good effect.

#310

You have to get rid of every possession you own, apart from what will fit in your school bag. What will you keep?

#311

In 10 years' time, the Mars One organisation hopes to send a group of humans to Mars to live there. Permanently.

Will you be signing up?

Also, what problems can you foresee with the idea of a one-way ticket to Mars? What sort of reasons might make someone want to take the trip?

#312

What is a soul?

#313

People don't write as many letters as they used to. Emails, texts, online messages and tweets are used much more often to get in contact instantly. The problem with these is that many of these get deleted as time goes on. A recent survey by Sainsbury's Bank[1] found that British people accidentally lost over 2 billion pieces of digital media content in a two-year period. Even if they're not deleted by accident, many photos nowadays are sitting on a hard drive, flash stick or uploaded to a website somewhere instead of being printed out.

In a hundred years' time, how will historians learn about life back in 2014?

Also, while you're thinking about it ...

Is there a difference in the content of digital records (like emails, texts, digital photos) compared with paper ones? In other words, do people take different sorts of photos or write different sorts of 'letters' because everything is much more immediate and disposable? Is this a good thing?

#314

The letters of the alphabet have been sorted into three groups. Can you spot the rule?

A B C D
E K M T U
V W Y

H I O X

F G J
L N P Q
R S Z

CLUES:

- Once you've got Group 2, the others will fall into place.
- It's got something to do with the shape of the letters rather than their sound or use.

1 See <http://sainsburysbankmedia.co.uk/brits-have-lost-1-billion-of-digital-media-content/>.

#315

A 93-year-old man, William Snell, wrote a great list of Life's Little Instructions. Here are some of them. Pick two to focus on today and five for the week.

TREAT EVERYONE YOU MEET LIKE YOU WANT TO BE TREATED

NEVER WASTE AN OPPORTUNITY TO TELL SOMEONE YOU LOVE THEM

LEAVE EVERYTHING A LITTLE BETTER THAN YOU FOUND IT

KEEP IT SIMPLE

THINK BIG THOUGHTS BUT RELISH SMALL PLEASURES

BECOME THE MOST POSITIVE AND ENTHUSIASTIC PERSON YOU KNOW

BE FORGIVING OF YOURSELF AND OTHERS

SAY 'THANK YOU' A LOT. SAY 'PLEASE' A LOT.

BE THE FIRST TO SAY 'HELLO'

RETURN ALL THINGS YOU BORROW

HAVE A DOG. ALWAYS ACCEPT AN OUTSTRETCHED HAND

BE THERE WHEN PEOPLE NEED YOU

DON'T BE AFRAID TO SAY 'I MADE A MISTAKE.' DON'T BE AFRAID TO SAY 'I DON'T KNOW.'

COUNT YOUR BLESSINGS

#316

There are plenty of words in other languages that mean things we don't have words for in English. Here are some definitions. Can you invent a new English word to sum them up?[1]

    a.   The extra weight you put on by eating when you're feeling fed up.

    b.   When you tap someone on the opposite shoulder from behind to fool them.

    c.   Not too much. Not too little. Just about right.

    d.   Scratching your head to help you remember something.

#317

What do you think is the greatest unsolved mystery ever?

#318

Don't ask yourself, 'How clever am I?' but instead, 'How am I clever?' Where do YOUR skills lie?

#319

How free are you? What is freedom?

#320

If you could choose to never go to sleep but never feel tired, would you?

Kahlo Class, Millennium Primary School, Greenwich

---

1 If you're interested, here are the languages that already have these words: a) German – *kummerspeck* (which, rather brilliantly, means 'grief bacon'!), b) Indonesian – *mencolek*, c) Swedish – *lagom* and d) Hawaiian – *pana po'o*.

#321

When Commander Chris Hadfield was in charge of the International Space Station, he tweeted lots of photographs of our planet from space.[1] Several of them were photos of what parts of Earth looked like as the sun set.

Whatever time you're reading this, wherever you are in the world, somewhere on Earth right now there's a sunset! As the International Space Station orbits the Earth once every 90 minutes, Commander Hadfield could see sunsets and sunrises all the time. So what time is it in space?

#322

What do people just not notice about you?

#323

'Unrelated things become interesting when we start fitting them together.'

John Kouwenhoven, English professor and author

Many creative people get their ideas from two objects or ideas that are put together in this way. The difference between those objects or the result when they are combined is where the fun part starts.

So, here are some unrelated words. Take two. Don't go for the obvious. What ideas can you come up with?

painting   fan   pack   words   run   safety   squirrel

For example, painting + squirrel = The red squirrel is a protected species in the UK because there are so few of them. What if we protected pieces of rare artwork by law too, so that they're never destroyed?

---

1 And played David Bowie songs. These weren't by any means the only things he did. But, perhaps unsur-prisingly, they are the most famous things he did.

sparky teaching

'If you think you are too small to make a difference, try sleeping in a closed room with a mosquito.' African Proverb

#324

How can YOU make a difference today?

148

#325

Technology is changing all the time. How can you keep your life private when there are so many ways to share it? Do you care?

#326

What is the most powerful job anyone could do? Think carefully ...

#327

'I am always doing what I cannot do yet, in order to learn how to do it.'
Vincent Van Gogh

What are you learning how to do?

#328

There are lots of computer applications now that allow you to tag photos or articles so that you can find them quickly. This isn't really a new idea when you think about it – some of our memories are triggered off by certain smells or sounds. The smell of a pine tree may bring Christmas flooding back or the taste of a roast dinner may remind you of your grandparents. Which memories do you have that are tagged with a smell? A sound? A texture?

#329

Which film has made you think the most?

#330

You know when you're typing on the computer and the spell checker autocorrects your spelling mistake with a word you didn't want to use? It's got a name – the Cupertino effect.

And you know when you're texting on your phone and the predictive text suggests the wrong word? That's got a name too – a textonym!

Here are some numbers that were pressed on a phone. Can you think of two possible words for each?

2665
4663
735328[1]

1	2 ABC	3 DEF
4 GHI	5 JKL	6 MNO
7 PQRS	8 TUV	9 WXYZ

#331

'If you're thankful for what you've got, you'll get more. If you concentrate on what you don't have, you'll never ever have enough.'

Have you got enough?

#332

You've been given a sabbatical from school for a month. You can do anything you like or go anywhere you like, but it must be educational. What will you do?

---

1 The last one might be too hard, but it's interesting because the two words are opposites. In both words the number 3 is always the letter E. Get it wrong and you could be sending out the wrong message, literally.

#333

At the University of Newcastle, a professor called Melissa Bateson once did an experiment. In the staff room was a box where members of staff would give money to pay for the tea and coffee they had drunk. One week Professor Bateson stuck a picture of some flowers above the honesty box, the next week she stuck a picture of some eyes, then it was back to flowers and so on. What she found was very interesting. On the weeks that she stuck the picture of the eyes above the honesty box, there was always more money than on the weeks where it was of flowers.

Why do you think this happened?

There is a book that talks about signs like this as being like little whistles to the butler inside your brain[1]. The things around us affect how we behave. Is there a similar experiment you can do in your school to test how the environment around you affects what you do?

---

1 If you're interested in this kind of thing, the book is *Thinking, Fast and Slow* by Daniel Kahneman (Penguin, 2012).

To be appreciated, place hand here:

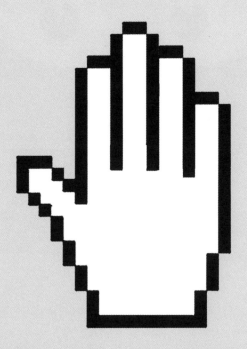

334

Who deserves a high five of thanks today from you? Give them one.

#335

Using only the letters on the top line of a QWERTY keyboard, what's the longest word you can make? (You can use the letters as many times as you like.)

#336

On 20 January, the people of the United States celebrate Martin Luther King Day. He was a man who spent most of his life working to make sure people were treated equally. His most famous speech contained the words: 'I have a dream ... ' Martin Luther King's big dream was for a world where all people were treated the same. What's YOUR big dream for the world? And how are you going to work to make it happen?

#337

Which is better – to write a fantastic story really messily or to write an average story in beautiful handwriting?

What do you think your teacher thinks? What *does* your teacher think?

#338

If you could alter a fictional character or the course of a story, what would you change and why?

#339

The fact you can read things on the Internet is mostly thanks to miles and miles of fibre-optic Internet cables deep under the sea. There are over 550,000 of them down there.

What if those cables broke and the Internet crashed?

Try not to think of only negative consequences. Would there be any positive effects?

'If we're all on the same team, let's start acting like it. We got work to do!'

- Kid President

Write a pep talk to get your class moving in the morning and to make the most of every day.

It's worth mentioning that the quote above comes from a video[1] made by Brad Montague and his nine-year-old brother-in-law, Robby Novak. They started off making videos for fun and still do, only now they get seen by millions and have taken them to the White House and United Nations. Robby (or Kid President as he is better known by most of the world!) has Osteogenesis Imperfecta, which means that he has had over 70 bone breaks since birth. Watch his videos in light of this and he'll not only inspire you with his words but his exceptional attitude. It's fair to say Robby Novak would be a pretty inspirational boy even if he had never been Kid President.

---

1 You can see it here: <http://www.youtube.com/watch?v=l-gQLqv9f4o>.

#341

People often talk about the fact that we are going to have to teach 'twenty-first-century skills' to solve 'twenty-first-century problems'. Many of the skills they mention aren't twenty-first-century at all – medieval knights had to be resilient and Roman soldiers had to be creative – but there are plenty of problems that are new. Here's one:

Twitter and Facebook are really useful for spreading the word quickly about missing people. Police departments often use them effectively. Last August, a police department in England tweeted about a missing little girl. Thankfully, later that day they tweeted that they had found her safe and well. But five days later, people were still retweeting the original information. If an old tweet of ours gets retweeted it's no problem, but for police and fire services it could be more important.

Presuming that emergency services don't want to delete their tweets and need them as a record, can you think of a way to solve this problem? Can you think of another twenty-first-century problem and a possible solution?

#342

What makes you irreplaceable? (In case you didn't already know, you are!)

#343

A note to teachers: this is a fairly risky question to put to your class but rewarding if you are open-minded enough to take on board the feedback. Teaching isn't primarily about student enjoyment, but it helps. Ask it to more mature pupils and you'll find out interesting facts about yourself and them.

You don't have to attend your teacher's classes any more. In fact, you can move to any other classroom in school for the next week. What is it about lessons in this particular classroom that would make you want to stay? What would put you off? How could your teacher sell their brand of teaching to you?[1]

---

1 This is loosely based on a fantastic question Dave Burgess asks in his inspirational book *Teach Like a Pirate* (Dave Burgess Consulting, 2012): 'If your students didn't have to be there, would you be teaching to an empty room?' Here in the UK, this book is not as well-known as it ought to be. You can find out more here: <http://daveburgess.com>.

#344 WHAT MAKES YOU YOU?

IS IT SOMETHING OUTSIDE OF YOU?

YOUR FAMILY? HOW MUCH OF YOU COMES FROM THE PEOPLE WHO BROUGHT YOU UP?

WHERE YOU LIVE? IF YOU'D BEEN BORN IN AFGHANISTAN OR UGANDA, HOW MUCH OF YOU WOULD STILL BE THE SAME?

YOUR FRIENDS? DOES THAT MEAN THAT WE'RE PRODUCTS OF WHO WE HANG OUT WITH AND YOUR PARENTS WERE RIGHT WHEN THEY SAID: 'YOU'RE HANGING OUT WITH THE WRONG CROWD'?

YOUR EXPERIENCES? HAS WHAT'S HAPPENED TO YOU AND HOW YOU'VE DEALT WITH IT MOULDED WHO YOU ARE?

OR
IS IT SOMETHING
INSIDE OF YOU?

YOUR BELIEFS?
WHAT DO YOU BELIEVE IN?

YOUR SOUL?
WHAT'S A SOUL?

YOUR THOUGHTS?
WHERE DO THEY COME FROM?

AND HOW IMPORTANT
IS KNOWING THE
ANSWER ANYWAY?

#345

In the North Sea, about six miles off the east coast of Britain, is a Second World War sea fort. HM Fort Roughs is made up of two concrete towers connected by a platform and was built as part of the British wartime sea defence just outside of British waters. In the 1950s it was abandoned, but in the late 1960s it was taken over and its new inhabitants declared it 'The Principality of Sealand'. Although the original Sealand inhabitant, Prince Roy, has now passed away, the 'nation' of Sealand still exists. Over the years it has issued its own passports and currency and even has its own national anthem.

If you were to start up your own country (which you can do if you have some undisputed territory to build on), what would it be like?

What differences would there be between your new country and your current one? What would you keep the same?

#346

Come up with three cures for procrastination.

#347

Your teammate yells out your name.

The sound travels in ripples through the air. The vibrating sound waves eventually reach you and, like some kind of satellite dish, your outer ears pick up the signal!

The sound waves travel down your ear canal. They then hit your eardrum, causing it to vibrate. This, in turn, makes three tiny bones vibrate (one of which is the smallest bone in your body), which causes fluid in your inner ear to vibrate. Finally, a message gets sent to your brain to turn around and catch the basketball they've just thrown.

This all happens in a split second.

WOW.

What everyday thing makes you say WOW?

#348

What would you like to tell the world about 'the youth of today'? That's you by the way!

#349

Can you use your imagination in maths? Can you set up experiments in music? Can science ever be poetic? Can there be a formula to art?

#350

Write three questions that might feature on the GCSE Common Sense exam paper.

#351

Why is the sky black at night time?

> Maple Tree Class, Tirlebrook Primary School, Gloucs

#352

Semordnilap (read it backwards!) are words that make different words when you read them backwards. So words like FLOW, WARTS, STRESSED and the name LEON are all semordnilaps. Which other words can you think of that make a different word when you read them backwards?

#353

A piece of cheese and the Mona Lisa. Which is more incredible? Why?

#354

NOTE TO OUR PUBLISHER :

SORRY - WE'RE NOT SURE WHAT THIS QUESTION WAS SUPPOSED TO BE. WE'RE FAIRLY SURE IT BEGAN WITH THE WORD 'INSTEAD', IT WAS ABOUT BRAINS, AND HAD A COMMA IN IT. IF YOU HAVE ANY IDEAS, PLEASE LET US KNOW.

THANKS.

#355

Thinking Outside of the Boxes

A lot of school is about fitting you into little boxes. If you're born between certain months of the year, you're put into a year group that you'll probably stay in for the rest of your school life.[1]

For most of your education your day is spent split up into chunks – one chunk for each subject that the authorities have decided are important for you to learn. And, at the end of your time at school, it is hoped that you leave with a set of qualifications that will help you on to the next stage of your life.

Can you think of any other way of organising things?

---

1 Did you know some people think that this 'year group' box that you're put into can affect your progress in some way? Often those who were born nearer to the start of a school year (e.g. those born in September in the UK) are more likely to be sports stars than those born nearer the end. This is probably to do with being that little bit taller and stronger than those born 10 months later. But (and this bit is important) don't let this piece of trivia stop you from going for it – Roger Federer and Andy Murray were two of the youngest in their classes.

#356

In the song 'High Hopes' (Van Heusen & Cahn, 1959), the lyrics talk about an ant who has so much self-belief, he thinks he can move a rubber tree plant.

What's your rubber tree plant?[1]

#357

Some cruise ships are like floating cities, having shops, gyms, cinemas and even clinics. They have to provide all sorts of facilities to keep travellers who may be on them for the best part of a year happy and healthy.

But with all these facilities, how do they still manage to float, when some people can't?

#358

One of the words of the year for 2013 was 'selfie'. But how about a shelfie?

Get some of your class and your teachers/kitchen staff/cleaners/caretaker to take a photo of their bookshelves.[2] What can you tell about them by their shelfies? Are you inspired to read any of the books they've got on there?

#359

People talk about building confidence, but then they complain if you're overconfident. Where's the line? How much confidence is enough?

#360

Are there any questions we'll never find the answer to? If so, is there any point asking them?

---

1 The thing that everyone says you can't do, but you'll prove them wrong by doing.
2 A note to teachers: when discussing this on Twitter, someone came up with the idea that a Spot-the-Shelfie display might be a good way of encouraging reluctant readers and providing good reading role models (particularly if you can involve your whole school community).

#361

Which lesson will always stick in your mind from the past year? What's the best way for your teacher to get a lesson to stick?

#362

When was the last time you REALLY pushed yourself?

#363

What strategies do you use to Keep Calm and Carry On in a crisis?

#364

Things look smaller the further away they are.

And, with time, some things can feel smaller than they once did.

What sorts of big things today will feel much smaller next week?

What sorts of things are so important they never really feel any smaller?

#365

The answer is

What was the question?

Answers

It was never our intention to put an answer page into this book. The whole point is to get you and your students thinking and what better way to do so than to encourage them to seek out the answers for themselves? In addition, most of the questions are open-ended anyway.

However, some of the Hmmms do have a right answer or benefit from additional explanations. Here they are:

#009

This is a typical investigation involving ordering digits. As with most investigations, the 'start small and get more complicated' rule will really help. Start with two brothers, then three etc. Once you've drawn a table, students may notice that each new total of positions is made by multiplying the previous total by the new number of brothers. Once you get to 4 brothers, it's time to stop listing the possibilities and just calculate them.

Number of brothers	Number of possibilities
1	1
2	2
3	6
4	24
5	120
6	720
7	5040

015

The year is 1987.

023

None of the facts are actually facts. we made them all up. So, how can you trust what you read? As Abraham Lincoln once said, 'Without checking every fact out there, how can you be sure what you read in a book or on the Internet is true?'[1]

028

The words are: STARTLING, STARTING, STARING, STRING, STING, SING, SIN, IN, I

038

These are the initial letters of numbers, so the next three letters are S, E, N (Seven, Eight, Nine).

043

Surely, the answer to this is 25% because there are four possible answers? But, as two of those answers say '25%', perhaps the chance of getting the right answer must actually be 2 out of 4 (or 50%).

If the answer's 50%, though, that means that only option B is right. So, we are back to 1 out of 4 again.

The truth is that this is a trick question and is just about getting you thinking about probability.

044

The letter Y first crops up in the number T-W-E-N-T-Y. It's a simple starter to lure you into the trickier question that follows. The first time the letter A appears is in the number O-N-E-H-U-N-D-R-E-D-A-N-D-O-N-E.

---

1 This is made up too.

060

There is no extra pound. This is a famous riddle and it's all about the way it's worded. It can be really confusing unless you follow the money carefully.

a. Shannon and Bailey pay £25 to the restaurant for the meal, which is £12.50 each.
£25 ÷ 2 = £12.50

b. They also give the waiter a £3 tip, which works out at £1.50 each.
£3 ÷ 2 = £1.50

c. So, the cost of their meal and the tip is £14.00 each.
£12.50 (meal) + £1.50 (tip) = £14.00
Shannon's mistake is when she says that they spent 'two fourteens' on their meals. This isn't true. They spent 'two fourteens' on their meals including the tip for the waiter.

d. The waiter gives them £2 back, which is £1 each. Having spent £14.00 on the meal and tip, £1 is exactly the change each person needs from the £15.00 they spent.

064

The least common digit is 0 which features 192 times.

Then come the digits 2-9 which feature 300 times.

The most common digit is 1 which features 301 times. Here's a question: where did the extra one come from? (Unlike the previous answer above, there is actually an extra one this time!)

068

Just to clarify, there is no right odd one out here. It's a question designed to see what you come up with.

075

There are quite a few to choose from, but an interesting way to use this question is to come up with at least one for each continent. For example:

Europe: SPAIN, Americas: CHILE, Oceania: SAMOA, Africa: GHANA, Asia: JAPAN

Others include Benin, China, Egypt, Ghana, Haiti, India, Italy, Kenya, Libya, Malta, Nepal, Qatar, Sudan, Syria, Tonga and Yemen. There are more.

#095

Start with Friday. Your head of year can't surprise you with a Friday detention because all the days will go by and then on Thursday night you'll know for definite it's going to be the next day. No surprise! So it can't be on Friday.

What about Thursday? Now that we've crossed out Friday, Thursday is now the last day in the week that it could be. So when it gets to Wednesday night, again you'll know for definite that it's going to be the next day. Once more, no surprise!

And so on. This is a famous philosophical question and the answer is that if you cross them off one by one, you'll never be surprised.

#110

astronomers – no more stars

funeral – real fun

united – untied

honestly – on the sly

silent – listen

violence – nice love

within earshot – I won't hear

forty-five – over fifty

restful – fluster

#117

A clue to solve the code: there is a one-letter word in the question. It can only be one of two words. Which is more likely? Once you've discovered that word, try and use it to help work out the other letters.

The answer: it's a number which is the digit 1 followed by 100 zeroes (or 10^{100}). Whilst you could write that number out fairly easily, you'd find it harder to show a 'googolplex' which is the digit 1 followed by a googol zeroes.

#120

The answer is 42 times. This may sound unbelievable, but when numbers are doubled they increase very quickly (also see #221 which is also about doubling).

#125

This isn't a trick question. The door to a bus always faces the pavement and is usually at the front of the bus. Think about what side of the road you drive on in your country and you'll be able to work out which direction it's going.

#127

This question is trickier than it looks. The lower numbers are harder to make than the higher ones. There may be other methods, but here are ways to make the minutes from 1-10. To make things easier, let's call the three minute timer, Timer A and the four minute one, Timer B.

1 minute: Turn both egg timers over. Stop them both after three minutes when Timer A runs out. You'll be left with one minute left in Timer B.

2 minutes: This is a tricky one. One method is to do what you did for 1 minute. Then, turn Timer A over at the same time as the one minute you have left in Timer B. When that minute runs out, stop Timer A immediately. One of the three minutes will have been used up, so you'll have two minutes of sand left in there.

3 minutes: Just use Timer A.

4 minutes: Just use Timer B.

5 minutes: Do what you did for two minutes. Time the two minutes and, when they are up, turn Timer A back over to add another three minutes.

6 minutes: Use Timer A twice in a row.

7 minutes: Use Timer A and then Timer B.

8 minutes: Use Timer B twice in a row.

9 minutes: Use Timer A three times in a row.

10 minutes: Use Timer A twice and then Timer B.

#128

The coincidences are due to the fact he was Louis the 14th. That number crops up a lot in his life.

    a. If you add the digits of the year he ascended to the throne, they make 14.

    b. If you add the digits of the year he died, they make 14.

    c. If you add the digits of his age when he died, they make 14.

    d. If you subtract 1643 from 1715, you'll see he reigned for 72 years. $7 \times 2 = 14$.

Another fact is that Louis was crowned king in May of 1643. The day? The 14th!

#136

Each new number is found by adding the last two numbers before it. 1+1 =2, 1+2=3 and so on. The next two numbers then are 13 (5+8) and 21 (8+13). These are called Fibonacci numbers after the man who introduced these numbers to Western mathematicians. What have they got to do with the spiral? Try starting in the middle and writing each number in the squares as they spiral out.

Students: Fibonacci numbers are really interesting and have a lot of links with nature. If you want to know more, here's a good place to start: <http://www.mathsis-fun.com/numbers/nature-golden-ratio-fibonacci.html>.

Teachers: you might be interested in Arthur Benjamin's TED talk on 'The magic of Fibonacci numbers' <http://www.ted.com/talks/arthur_benjamin_the_magic_of_fibonacci_numbers>.

#140

The ball is thrown upwards. Gravity brings it back downwards without it touching anything.

#148

Here are the facts:

On average, unprovoked sharks attack somewhere between 50 and 80 people every year. Of these, usually less than 10 people are killed. Mosquitoes (and the subsequent spread of malaria) are responsible for around 655,000 deaths a year, mostly in Africa. On average, elephants kill at least 200 people every year.

So why is it that the subject of many scary films and the creature you are probably most fearful of, is the shark?

#153
It's the letter F...

#158
The only time this looks like it might not work is when you add the two digits together and they make a two-digit number. What do you do then? Put both digits in the middle? For example 28 x 11. 2+8 = 10 so you could write 2108 as the answer, but it would be wrong. It does work, however, if you remember your place value columns and think of the 1 as going underneath the 2.

$$28 \times 11 \qquad 2 + 8 = 10$$

3 0 8   ... so the answer is 308.

#165
All the facts were true, but this was a slightly trick question. The time machine is a normal wardrobe. If you want to travel in time three hours into the future, you can just go and sit in there for three hours. We all travel through time every day.

171

#177

This is based on a famous philosophical question. The best answer to say is 'No'. Here's why:

If you say 'Yes' and you're right, you'll keep your job. But if you're wrong, that means that he is going to fire you.

If you say 'No' and you're right, you should keep your job because you answered correctly. If you say 'No' and you're wrong, you should still have a job because he wasn't planning to fire you anyway.

#184

These numbers were picked at random and there are probably lots of ways to get there. Here's one:

$$9 + 5 = 14$$
$$14 \times 50 = 700$$
$$25 + 6 = 31$$
$$700 + 31 = 731$$

Here's the same thing using brackets:

$$50 (9 + 5) + (25 + 6)$$

#190

A clue: try halving it a few times.

If you halve 1,000,000 six times, you get the answer 15625 which doesn't have any zeroes in it.

So that means, if you start with 15625 and double it six times, you'll get one million. Doubling it once is the same as x2, doubling twice is the same as x4 and so on. If you keep going, you'll work out that doubling six times is just the same as x64. So the way to make one million using your calculator is by multiplying 15625 by 64.

#193

The house is at the North Pole. Any direction you look when you're at the North Pole is South.

#203

As Henry Ford's quote suggests, ATTITUDE is 100%!

#207

The number of gifts on each day are all triangular numbers (1 on Day One, 3 on Day Two, 6 on Day Three and so on). If you add these together for the twelve days, you should end up with 364. A gift for every day of the year except Christmas.

#214

This is a question of logic. If Pinocchio is telling the truth, then his nose is really long. But if his nose is long, that means he's lying. If he's lying when he says his nose is long, it must be short. But then it can't be short because it grows when he tells lies. And so on.

#221

Hopefully you made a prediction for how long it would take. Seven billion is a big number and you probably chose quite a few years. But if we start with 1 person, the next day there will be 2 people and the next day there will be 4 people. And what do we know about numbers when they double? (see answer #120 above). They get very big very quickly.

Here are the numbers:

1 2 4 8 16 32 64 128 256 512 1024 2048 4096 8192 16,384 32,768 65,536 131,071 262,144 524,288 1,048576 2,097,152 4,194,304 8,388,608 16,777,216 33,554,432 67,108,864 134,217,728 268,435,456 536,870,912 1,073,741,824 (that's just over one billion) 2,147,483,648 4,294,967,296 8,589,934,592 (that's over eight and a half billion)

So, if you count them all up, we've got to eight and a half billion people tagged in only 34 days of playing the game.

222

There is one word longer than any you have found. According to the Internet, apparently SGIOMLAIREACHED is actually a word given to describe the habit of dropping in at mealtimes.

227

The word is 'et', the Latin for 'and'. Now have a go at designing your own ampersand based on 'et'.

234

There are lots of possible answers to this question. Here's one:

12+3+4+5-6-7+89=100

There are at least another two that start with the number 12, four that start with the number 1 and three that start with the number 123. What are they?

249

The wrds are as fllws: outdoor, obnoxious, octopus, onlooker, opposition, voodoo, cockatoo, canoe, occasional

This could be extended by getting your students to come up with a similar question, but using a different broken letter. They could even not inform others what their missing letter is, although this might prove too difficult.

255

The hands sit on top of each other at one point every hour, but with this question, remember that the hour hand moves slightly with each minute. So, 'half past six' isn't actually true. It would probably be more like thirty three minutes past six as the hour hand would have moved halfway between the six and the seven.

265

The words are ILL BEE CAT (or ACT!) TEN (or NET!) and WOW.

277
Depending on the definition you use, space officially begins 100km (or 62 miles) directly upwards from Earth. So, it might surprise you to find out that it would only take you an hour to drive up to space if you travelled at at 60mph.

284
KEEP OUT! NO SKATEBOARDING ALLOWED.

KEEP OUT? NO! SKATEBOARDING ALLOWED.

296
arm, leg, ear, eye, jaw, toe, rib, lip, hip, gum

314
This question is all about symmetry. The letters in the first group have one line of symmetry, the second group have more than one line of symmetry and the final group have no lines of symmetry.

330
2665 – book, cool

4663 - good, hood, home, hoof, gone

735328 - select, reject

335
The QWERTY keyboard was set out in non-alphabetical order so that typists didn't have to keep unjamming their typewriters because common letters were sitting next to each other. Apparently, to enable typewriter salesmen to type a word quickly and show off the wonders of their new product, the letters for that particular word were put in the top row. And so, one of the longest words you can make using just the top row is TYPEWRITER.

A Hmmm-Dex

This list is by no means exhaustive, but may be useful in locating questions that fit a specific skill you wish to develop.

A sense of awe and wonder about the world:
006, 010, 034, 130, 131, 170, 208, 304, 347, 353,

Big things:
076, 091, 178, 226, 228, 241, 269, 285, 287, 306, 307, 312, 319

Character:
003, 017, 030, 032, 101, 114, 115, 126, 143, 172, 175, 213, 359

Creativity:
002, 011, 012, 040, 054, 116(a+b), 156, 162, 191, 216, 238, 291, 323

Learning and school-life:
013, 020, 056, 072, 073, 074, 199, 235, 245, 263, 281, 297, 308, 343, 355, 361

Literacy skills:
025, 033, 050, 089, 163, 192, 216, 249, 272

Logical and strategic thinking:
043, 177, 183, 214, 243, 274,

Mathematical thinking:
009, 037, 083, 120, 127, 128, 136, 147, 158, 184, 190, 207, 221, 234, 252

Personal/Inter-personal skills:
008, 080, 081, 107, 266, 267, 334, 344

sparky teaching

Positive thinking:
035, 052, 073, 098, 132, 174, 203, 340, 356

Problem-solving:
060, 117, 125, 140, 153, 229, 277, 314, 330, 341

Further reading to make you go Hmmm ...

In the writing of 365 Things, we have deliberately avoided fantastic resources like Ian Gilbert's 'Thunks' in order to try and ensure our ideas were as original as possible. If you like this book, you may appreciate the following:

365 Things To Make You Go Hmmm ...
<sparkyteaching.com/resources/thinkingskills/hmmm.php> Website.

Burgess, Dave. **Teach Like a Pirate: Increase Student Engagement, Boost Your Creativity, and Transform Your Life as an Educator**. Dave Burgess Consulting Inc, 2012. Print.

Gilbert, Ian. **Independent Thinking**. Independent Thinking Press, 2014. Print.

Gilbert, Ian. **The Little Book of Thunks: 260 Questions to Make Your Brain Go Ouch!** Independent Thinking Press, 2007. Print.

Kahneman, Daniel. **Thinking: Fast and Slow**. Penguin, 2012. Print.

McFall, Dr Matthew. **The Little Book of Awe and Wonder: A Cabinet of Curiosities**. Independent Thinking Press, 2013. Print.

Poundstone, William. **Are You Smart Enough to Work at Google?** Oneworld Publications, 2013. Print.

Reynolds, Peter H. **Ish**. Walker Books, 2005. Print.

Reynolds, Peter H. **The Dot**. Walker Books, 2004. Print.

Roberts, Hywel. **Oops! Helping children learn accidentally**. Independent Thinking Press, 2012. Print.

sparky teaching

Waters, Mick. **Thinking Allowed: On Schooling**. Independent Thinking Press, 2013. Print.

Worley, Peter (ed.). **The Philosophy Shop**. Independent Thinking Press, 2012. Print.

SPARKY TEACHING WOULD LIKE TO THANK...

... OUR PUBLISHERS:

Ian Gilbert who suggested the idea of turning 365 Things into a book and giving Sparky Teaching a chance to be published.

Caroline Lenton and her Independent Thinking Press team who have helped to make the process easier and lived up to their promise of providing 'your voice in print'.

Rosalie Williams whose supply of Independent Thinking books over the years has provoked several of the questions here.

... OUR SCHOOL CONTRIBUTORS:
Eirian Painter (Deputy Head at Liberty Primary School, Merton) – as well as Andrew Kite – for taking the 365 Things idea and using it so successfully across their whole school.

Those who have submitted work that features here – Miss Thomas' English Class at Oldfields Hall Middle School and Pete Jones' Year 8 students at Les Quennevais School.

... OUR COMPETITION WINNERS:
We ran a competition on the website to submit questions. The following classes' entries were selected to feature in the book. Well done!
> Y4, Rickmansworth Park JMI School, Hertfordshire
> P6b, Cornbank St James Primary School, Penicuik
> Kahlo Class, Millennium Primary School, Greenwich
> Matthew, Birch Class, Liberty Primary School, Merton
> Tiffany, Cedar Class, Liberty Primary School, Merton
> Mr Woodburn's Class, Year 4, Milnthorpe Primary School, Cumbria
> P7, St Margaret's Primary, Cowie
> Maple Tree Class, Tirlebrook Primary School, Gloucs.

... AND FINALLY:
Most importantly, to our families who have supported, encouraged and inspired us. Specifically to 365 Things, to those who have suggested questions and ideas: our parents, Aled, Andrew, Dawn, Jane, Mark, Michele and Nan.

Things that've made you go Hmmm...

Things that've made you go  Hmmm...

Praise for 365 Things To Make You Go Hmmm...

Whatever you do, don't buy this book! At least, not if you want to be remotely productive, focused or are required to feed a small child regularly. *365 Things To Make You Go Hmmm...* entertains, inspires, frustrates, befuddles, baffles and amuses in equal measure. Although the concept is to use one Thing per day, it is impossible to not read on, wrestle with a Thing, read on, wrestle with another Thing ... You know this book has you completely hooked when you can hear your own brain arguing with itself!

From the challenging, and in some ways uncomfortable, introduction, *365 Things* sparks your thinking into life by making you reflect on the values and messages that you give learners. For example, how many times have we said (even though we hate the thought of it), 'Only 105 days until SATs'? Most of us have done it, not through some sadistic pleasure of piling stress onto young learners, but as a reflection of the externally induced pressures we're put under. Maybe this book will go some way to alleviating this. By embedding the messages, values and prompts contained in *365 Things,* we'd get deeper thinking, self-valuing, confident learners ready to take on the world, secure in the knowledge that they're all good at what really counts and see SATs (and other tests) as an opportunity to show those in power just how great they are.

The 365 Things themselves cover a wide range of topics and concepts, and are in some ways similar to 'Thunks', but the Sparky Teaching flavour is unmistakable: lots of values-based content, with practical tips and tricks to extend and augment the learning, all done in a positive, light-hearted way. A particular strength of this book is how 'real life' has been used to develop some of the Things (e.g. news stories, web content) increasing relevance for your learners, and many Things are cleverly illustrated, with the presentation adding an extra 'must-read' dimension.

365 Things, despite seemingly limiting itself to only one year's use, will undoubtedly impact on you and your learners for years to come. Aside from the value-instilling content, the Things will stimulate enough additional questions and thinking that you could end up writing your own book! (This probably isn't the result the publishers wanted though, so don't tell them I told you!)

With this book in your collection, you'll have a ready-made source of stimulating content that can be used for everything from whole-school assemblies through to class debates and corridor displays. And if you do work out if street dancing is a sport, let me know!

Paul Bannister, Head Teacher, Highbank Primary School

At the Northern Rocks Conference in May 2014, Debra Kidd talked about designing 'a curriculum with a conscience' and suggested that we ask ourselves, 'Is the child being asked to consider big questions?' If, as a teacher, school leader or parent, you are committed to the principle that this should happen in your classroom/school/home, this book will be a terrific resource.

Its gentle humour, its flexibility (which gives you the scope to use it in your own way and to suit your context) and its focus on values, imagination and creativity will ensure that it sparks 'awe and wonder'. It will stimulate your curiosity and then suggests useful links so that you can follow up your interests. It will help children to discover talents and passions they didn't know they had, and encourage them to be the best they can be – within the classroom and beyond it.

If you are searching for interesting facts and big questions to intrigue you, to make you think, to challenge you (whatever your age) and to stimulate fascinating discussion at school or at home, then *365 Things To Make You Go Hmmm...* is an excellent place to start.

Jill Berry, Former Head Teacher and Educational Consultant

Before reading *365 Things To Make You Go Hmmm...*, I hadn't realised that I'd been on Earth for 1.3 billion seconds, and I'd never thought about what someone would feel like after spending a day in my mind. That's the beauty of this incredible book – it asks you to think about things that you've probably never thought about before. The questions are great for starting classroom discussions, but they also work well for starting a conversation between a parent and child.

365 Things To Make You Go Hmmm... is an amazing resource. Chock full of questions about maths, logic, crosswords and introspection, it made my head hurt – but in a good way!

I highly recommend this book for any teacher, parent or curious individual.

Patrick Vennebush, Author, *Math Jokes 4 Mathy Folks*